TECHNIQUES AND RESOURCES IN TEACHING GRAMMAR

TEACHING TECHNIQUES IN ENGLISH AS A SECOND LANGUAGE
Series Editors: Russell N. Campbell and William E. Rutherford

TECHNIQUES AND RESOURCES IN TEACHING GRAMMAR

Marianne Celce-Murcia
Sharon Hilles

· OXFORD UNIVERSITY PRESS ·

1988

Oxford University Press

200 Madison Avenue, New York, NY 10016 USA
Walton Street, Oxford OX2 6DP England

Library of Congress Cataloging-in-Publication Data
Celce-Murcia, Marianne.
   Techniques and resources in teaching grammar.
   (Teaching techniques in English as a second
language)
   Bibliography: p.
   Includes index.
   1. English language–Study and teaching–Foreign
speakers. 2. English language–Grammar–Study and
teaching. I. Hilles, Sharon. II. Title. III. Series.
PE1128.A2C394   1987   428'.007   87-23948
ISBN 0-19-434191-7 (pbk.)

Printing: 10 9 8 7 6 5 4 3 2

Printed in Hong Kong.

To Daniel and George

· CONTENTS ·

·ACKNOWLEDGMENTS·

We are indebted to many friends and colleagues for their assistance to us in the preparation of this volume.

First of all, Russ Campbell and Bill Rutherford, the series editors, have given us useful feedback and suggestions during all phases of the project, as have Susan Lanzano, our editor, Mary Lynne Nielsen, associate editor, and Jeanne Rabenda and Cindi Di Marzo, assistant editors, at Oxford University Press. We are most grateful to all six of them for helping us at every turn.

Secondly, we owe special thanks to Jan Eyring, our colleague at UCLA, for giving us the benefit of her thorough and constructive suggestions on our first draft, as well as doing a structure index for that draft, which greatly assisted us in preparing the index for this version.

Third, we very much appreciate the illustrations that a fellow ESL teacher, Randall Burger, prepared for the pilot version of the manuscript. This enabled us to pilot the materials in a realistic form, and later these illustrations provided excellent models for the artists at Oxford University Press.

Others we would like to thank are: Ken Sheppard, editorial consultant, who made many useful suggestions for the final draft; Joan Samara, who typed several chapters of the first draft so that they would be duplicable for the piloting; and Caroline Celce-Murcia, who helped lend authenticity to several of our texts.

Our final thanks goes to friends and colleagues, whose work in research and teaching is very much reflected in this volume, for we are very aware that much of what we have suggested does not originate with us. The list is too long to mention everyone, but we must acknowledge at least the following people: Mike Gasser, Evelyn Hatch, Marilyn Hulquist, Diane Larsen-Freeman, Sadae Iwataki, Michael

I

Long, Dale McIntire, Carol Pomeroy, John Povey, Jack Richards, Fred Rosensweig, Bob Rumin, Barbara Schumann, John Schumann, Peter Shaw, Susan Stern, James Taylor, Tracy Terrell, Ellyn Waldman, and the students in English 122K, winter quarter 1986 at UCLA, who were the pilot group of "teachers-in-training" using these materials.

M. C-M.
S. H.   September, 1987
Los Angeles

·CHAPTER ONE·
Basic Issues

BACKGROUND

Of the many issues surrounding the teaching of grammar, perhaps the most controversial is whether to teach it at all. From an historical perspective, this controversy should come as somewhat of a surprise: teaching grammar has been central to and often synonymous with teaching foreign language for the past 2,500 years (Rutherford 1987). This tradition notwithstanding, in the past several years many ESL professionals have come to assume that second-language (L-2) learning is very much like first-language (L-1) acquisition. Their argument is that providing "comprehensible input" (language addressed to the learner that he or she can understand) is really all that a foreign- or second-language teacher can or should do to facilitate acquisition. According to Richards (1985:43), the basic assumption of such an approach is that " 'communicative' classrooms provide a better environment for second-language acquisition than classrooms dominated by formal instruction." It is not at all surprising that approaches like these have met with such enthusiasm; they are intuitively very appealing. Yet Richards warns that all too often techniques and approaches aren't based on actual evidence but rather

> . . . are promoted and justified through reference to intuitively appealing assertions and theories, which when repeated by those in positions of authority assume the status of dogma. (p. 43)

Richards goes on to point out that no actual empirical studies have been conducted that prove that "communicative" classrooms produce better language learners than the more traditional teacher-dominated classrooms. In fact, in spite of its intuitive appeal and the anecdotal

1

evidence which supports it, there is equally appealing and convincing evidence that a communicative approach can lead to the development of a broken, ungrammatical, pidginized form of the language beyond which students can never really progress. Such students are said to have "fossilized" in their acquisition of the language.

Part of the anecdotal evidence Richards refers to is a paper by Higgs and Clifford (1982). Before discussing their work, perhaps we should first review the Foreign Service Institute Oral Interview, a proficiency exam developed by the Foreign Service Institute Language Testing Unit. This examination, referred to by many as the FSI, is used by numerous foreign affairs agencies of the U.S. government. Although the FSI can measure both oral and reading skills, we are primarily concerned with the oral exam. The procedures for rating an individual on the FSI are exceedingly sophisticated and complex, and require a great deal of training. Thus, its administration is problematical. In spite of this, the FSI still yields the best assessment of oral proficiency that we know of. Its rating scale encompasses a wide range of proficiency levels from 0 to 5. Level 1 indicates minimal communicative competence; Level 5 designates the speech of an educated native speaker. In order ". . . to demonstrate to Americans having limited experience with foreign language what they themselves might sound like to a foreigner when attempting to communicate in the foreign language," Higgs and Clifford contrived the following examples of speech at each level.

Level	Visa Officer's Reply to Applicant
5	Under U.S. statutes, your affiliation with the Communist Party renders you ineligible for a regular tourist visa. There exist, however, waiver procedures which may be invoked. These are the steps that you should initiate . . .
4	According to U.S. lawss your affiliation wiz ze Communist Party makes you uneligible for a regular tourist visa. You may, however, request a waiver. Zis iss what you must do . . .
3	Zee laaw zayz zat mambears of zee Communistic Partee caanoht bee geeven a regoolair tooreest veesaa. Owehvair, egzeptions are zohmtaymes dunn. You must do zees . . .

2   You cannot legulally get toolist visa. It is not light, because
        berong to Communistic Palty. But you can ask for a special
        permission. You to do this . . .

1   You commyunist. No gyet vyisa. Got tryy agyain. Take thyis.
        Fyill in, plyeez. (p. 64)

As a result of their experience at the Defense Language Institute
and informal contacts at other governmental agencies such as the CIA
and the FSI, Higgs and Clifford identify a student type which they
call the "terminal 2/2 + ." This is a learner who cannot progress beyond
the rating of 2 or 2 + on the FSI exam. At this level, an individual com-
municates fluently but ungrammatically, though he often has a large
vocabulary. Apparently, the "terminal 2/2 +," (i.e., the student who
gets stuck at that level) is a prevalent phenomenon. Even highly
motivated and educated individuals aspiring to international careers
in government or management that require proficiency in a foreign
language sometimes fall into this category. Higgs and Clifford provide a profile of the "terminal 2/2 + ":

> This pattern of high vocabulary and low grammar is a classic
> profile of a terminal 2/2 + . . . It is important to note that the
> grammar weaknesses that are typically found in this profile are
> not *missing* grammatical patterns, which the student could learn
> or acquire later on, but are *fossilized* incorrect patterns. Ex-
> perience has shown again and again that such *fossilized* patterns
> are not remediable, even in intensive language training programs
> or additional in-country living experience. Hence the designa-
> tion *terminal 2/2 +* . . . The data suggest that members of the
> group that have arrived at the 2/2 + level through street learn-
> ing or through "communication first" programs are either un-
> successful at increasing their linguistic ability or tend to show
> improvement only in areas in which they had already shown
> high profiles . . . Members of the group that have arrived at
> the 2/2 + level through "accuracy first" programs, however,
> typically show the opposite prognosis. (pp. 67, 74)

In addition to the work by Higgs and Clifford, there have been numerous studies which suggest that comprehensible input is not enough to achieve high proficiency. Michael Long has pointed out that the data from these studies suggest that the prognosis in the long run is much better for those with overt formal instruction than for those with none.[1] Although these studies are highly suggestive and even persuasive, they are certainly far from conclusive. Indeed, as far as we know, there is insufficient direct evidence on either side to state categorically the effects of formal instruction on second-language learning. The jury is still out, but the question is being vigorously pursued by Long and his colleagues at the University of Hawaii, as well as others.

It is important to note that, to our knowledge, there are no studies that provide evidence that overt grammar instruction is essential. The burden of proof rests on those who maintain that grammar instruction is irrelevant to language acquisition, and so far no empirical support has been provided to support that claim. Although comprehensible input may be necessary, it is by no means clear that it is sufficient for mastery of a second language.

Let us now turn to a very practical argument in favor of teaching grammar, namely that many ESL/EFL students are required to pass a standardized national or international exam in order to proceed with their plans. These exams can determine their acceptance to a university or affect their professional or vocational advancement. These exams may even decide which professions are open to them. In other words, to one degree or another, their futures can be determined by their performance on an exam. Typically, a major component of such exams is grammar. Therefore, to give these students an incomplete grounding in grammar, regardless of one's conviction about teaching it, is to do them a great disservice. Students have to know and apply the rules of English grammar in order to do well on such tests.[2]

LEARNER VARIABLES

Although we are reluctant to abandon grammar teaching without

---

[1] Lecture given at UCLA on February 14, 1986.
[2] For an introduction to language testing as well as an idea of how language tests seek to measure grammatical competence, see Madsen (1983).

further evidence, we hestitate to recommend a single approach or method, as students have different learning strategies or styles. Studies in educational psychology suggest that people learning anything— including second or foreign languages—use at least two distinct strategies: analytical and holistic.[3] Analytical learners form and test hypotheses: consciously or unconsciously, they extract paradigms and rules from examples. Holistic learners, on the other hand, learn best by doing little or no analysis. Instead, they learn by exposure to large chunks of language in meaningful contexts. In second-language acquisition, these two types of learners might be designated as "rule learners" and "data gatherers" (Hatch, *et al.* 1985: 44). To complicate matters further, learning strategies are affected by age and task type. Children seem to prefer a holistic approach over an analytical one, and even those adults who are generally more comfortable with an analytical style often approach a completely new learning situation holistically and later switch to an analytical style. Additional information regard- ing learner differences has been reported by Hartnett (1985), and her findings suggest that deductive learning is more effective for students with left-hemispheric dominance (perhaps what we call analytical learners) and that inductive learning is as effective or more effective for those with right-hemispheric dominance (possibly what we call holistic learners). It seems, then, that if ESL teachers adopt a methodology which favors either a holistic or an analytical approach, or favors in- ductive reasoning over deductive reasoning, the odds are that they will not be equally effective with all of their students. In other words, it is probably the case that students do best in classes in which the teacher varies the approach in order to accommodate all learning styles.

We also know that some learners prefer visually-oriented gram- mar instruction (e.g., contextualized examples, sentences on the board or in a textbook) while others respond better to auditory input (e.g., listening to the same sentences being spoken, perhaps several times). Any approach that is either primarily visual, such as grammar transla- tion, or primarily auditory, such as the audio-lingual method, works against the natural learning preferences of some students. To prevent this lack of differentiation, we favor an approach to teaching grammar

[3] See Cronbach and Snow (1977), Witkin, *et al.* (1977) among others.

which encourages learners to use their eyes, their ears, and as many of the other senses as possible.

Another consideration is age. Lenneberg (1967) and others after him have found evidence pointing to a "critical period" for language acquisition. Although the critical period hypothesis has undergone various modifications and revisions, it essentially posits a period during which a child is biologically predisposed to language acquisition. During this period, the child learns whatever language(s) he is exposed to "automatically," without instruction or correction, provided the environment is linguistically rich enough.[4] Such a hypothesis could certainly account for the differences ESL teachers routinely observe between their adult learners and the learners' children. Regardless of the age limits set to define the critical period—and there is controversy over the precise limits—most researchers seem to agree that overt instruction in the L-1 during this period is of no value to the child and may even tend to slow the process of acquisition (Aitchison 1985). This might also apply to children learning an L-2 during the critical period. Thus, attempting to teach language—including grammar— may be not only futile but even detrimental in the long run.

The issue of children aside, not everyone can learn grammar; nor for that matter does everyone need to. For many of our learners, a pidginized communicative interlanguage is completely sufficient for their social and vocational needs. In such cases, a lexical approach as suggested by Schumann (1987) or a grammarless communicative syllabus may be the most efficient. It is a good idea, however, to inform students of the suspected effects of such a curriculum or approach. As Higgs and Clifford point out:

> While the most efficient way to achieve survival level proficiency would be a course that stressed vocabulary, our experience indicates that such a course would work to the disadvantage of students who wished to develop higher levels of proficiency. Students entering such a program would have to be warned of its potentially negative effect on their long-range aspirations. (p. 73)

[4] Aitchison (1985), Gleitman (1986), Hyams (1986), Landau and Gleitman (1985), Lightfoot (1983), among others.

Unfortunately, many learners arrive in classrooms having already achieved a fossilized pidgin, and frankly, the prognosis for their attaining native-like proficiency is not good, regardless of the amount of grammar instruction received. Still others, because of prior education, cognitive development, or age, are simply not able to master a foreign-language grammar. For these students, grammar instruction may not be as important as it is for others. It is interesting to note, however, that many of these students *demand* grammar instruction because it fulfills a cultural expectation of what constitutes a language class. Furthermore, it may be necessary for people who require native-like or near native-like proficiency (those learning English for professional or academic purposes, especially in the humanities, or those seeking assimilation into the target society). As Higgs and Clifford point out, "Survival and social integration bear little resemblance to each other" (p. 61). If a student's goal is the latter, grammar is important, if not absolutely essential.

Finally, it should be noted that learners will never truly attend to form unless they want to and are able to. They will learn best once they have achieved basic comprehension and can accept feedback on the form of their production in meaningful discourse, either spoken or written. In other words, feedback on form becomes more important after the student has acquired minimal competence and can absorb this feedback.

TEACHER PREPARATION

As we have noted, the questions of when and how to teach grammar depend on many variables. Students' needs change over the course of several weeks, and a teacher should be sensitive to these changes.

Regardless of a teacher's methodological preferences, a knowledge of grammar is essential to the ESL/EFL teaching professional. Such knowledge helps in carrying out several important and fundamental responsibilities:
• integrating form, meaning, and content in syllabus design
• selecting and preparing materials and classroom activities
• identifying and analyzing which student errors to concentrate on at any given time

- selecting and sequencing the grammatical forms to emphasize at any given time
- preparing appropriate exercises and activities for rule presentation or error correction
- answering students' questions about grammar

GRAMMAR AND OTHER LANGUAGE FACTORS

If grammar instruction is deemed appropriate for a class, the teacher's next step is to integrate grammar principles into a communicative framework, since the fundamental purpose of language is communication.[5] Unfortunately, grammar is often taught in isolated, unconnected sentences that give a fragmented, unrealistic picture of English and make it difficult for students to apply what they have learned in actual situations. Realistic and effective contextualization of an isolated grammar point is not always easy, but on the next few pages we would like to offer some suggestions we have found helpful.

First of all, there is a strong tendency for grammar or structural points to occur with one of three other aspects of language:[6]
- social factors
- semantic factors
- discourse factors

To help illustrate this tendency, let's consider each of these factors in detail.

Social Factors

"Social factors" refer to the social roles of interlocutors, their relationship to each other, and the purpose of the communication. Communicative functions such as requesting, inviting, refusing, agreeing, or disagreeing are all very sensitive to social factors such as politeness, directness, etc. For example, in refusing a request, the words and grammatical structures used depend on two basic variables: how well the individuals know each other and their social roles *vis-à-vis* one another.

---

[5] See Newmeyer (1983) for other uses.
[6] The basis for this framework was first suggested to us by Diane Larsen-Freeman.

The following are different ways of refusing a dinner invitation, but not all are equally appropriate for all situations:

a. Aww, I can't. I've gotta work.

b. Oh, I'm sorry; I'd love to, but I won't be able to. I have to work.

c. How nice of you to ask! I'd really be delighted, but I'm afraid I have to work that night.

The complexity of modals (e.g., *can*) and periphrastic modals (e.g., *have to, be able to*) lies in part in their social-interactional character: their use is socially constrained. Many ESL/EFL students find them difficult because they are frequently taught from a somewhat artificial semantic perspective rather than a social-interactive one. For example, teachers sometimes provide isolated semantic equivalents such as, "*Should* means an obligation or suggestion." The students are then perplexed at the reactions they provoke in their teacher when they *suggest* that he should go on a diet or modify his behavior in some way. If the use of a structure is constrained socially, situational factors, matters of personal choice, social functions, register differences, and other socio-linguistic variables come into play. As students become aware of these constraints, they learn that many suggestions are often inappropriate and even offensive in English.

Semantic Factors

These involve meaning. Grammatical structures that are most natually taught from a semantic perspective include expressions of time, space, degree, quantity, and probability. For example, the difference between the quantifiers *few* and *a few* in the following two sentences is primarily semantic:

a. John has a few good ideas.

b. John has few good ideas.

In (a), the emphasis is positive, while in (b) it is negative. The choice of a form is not governed by whom one is addressing, but rather by what one wants to say. Thus, the difference between *few* and *a few* is not illuminated by social-interactional factors because the difference between (a) and (b) does not rest on social factors but depends crucially on meaning. Therefore, expressions of location, time, space, degree, quantity, probability, etc. can be taught most effectively with a focus

on morphological, lexical, and syntactic contrasts that signal a difference
in meaning.

Discourse Factors

Our third category includes notions such as topic continuity, word
order, and the sequencing of new and old information. These factors
affect the forms that propositions take in the context of a discourse.
For example, indirect object movement in the following two sentences
is discourse governed (i.e., the decision to use one sentence or the other
depends on discourse factors). In English, we tend to put the most important element or the one on which we are focusing at the end of the
sentence. Hence the difference between (a) and (b) is one of focus.

    a. He gave the flowers to Mary.

      (Not to Janet, not to Carol. This might be in response to
      the question, "Who did he give the flowers to?")

    b. He gave Mary the flowers.

      (Not the candy, not the book. This might be in response to
      the question, "What did he give Mary?")

Another example is the use of logical connectors such as *even
though*, *although*, or *unless*. Our experience and that of many of our
colleagues suggests that defining these words semantically is less than
satisfying and often leads to a great deal of frustration and confusion
for both students and teacher. On the other hand, giving students a
portion of discourse which illustrates how these logical connectors function in context or what they signal in discourse seems to work remarkably
well. In other words, a definition of *although* may not be as helpful
as several sentences in which *although* is used, such as:

    a. Although John didn't study, he passed the test.

    b. Although Maria doesn't have much money, she is rich in
      spirit.

Our final category, then, consists of words and elements of language
which are more effectively defined or explained with reference to their
function in discourse than to their socio-linguistic function or semantic content.

All of these factors (i.e., social, semantic, discourse) interact with
each other, as well as with the structure of the language. Clearly there
are instances in which they overlap. They are not so much discrete

categories as continuous tendencies along multidimensional continua. But grammar instruction should always involve the matching of a structure or grammatical point with one of these three aspects of language; if that match can be made in preparing the grammar lesson and it captures a natural tendency in the language, the lesson will be easier for the teacher to prepare and easier for students to understand.

TECHNIQUES

Just as grammar points seem to pair naturally with other aspects of language, teaching techniques should vary according to the match being emphasized. For example, in structural-social matches such as modals and requests, the degree of politeness depends on the social relationship between the speaker and his or her interlocutor. In such cases, dramatization and other dynamic, interactional techniques allow learners to make the connection between structure and social function. Such techniques facilitate a proper match between the grammar point being presented and the language factor with which its use is most often associated.

On the other hand, if one is teaching quantifiers, locative prepositions, or modals of logical probability—structure-meaning matches—the most useful techniques are demonstration, illustration, and TPR activities.[7] These techniques allow the teacher to focus on meaning distinctions by manipulating the environment, thereby helping students to focus on contrasts, semantic systems such as sets or scales, or certain operations such as negation or inversion. These activities are more static than roleplay or dramatization, but they help students match linguistic form with semantic variables.

Finally, with structure-discourse matches, the major techniques include text generation, manipulation, and explanation. A combination of the teaching activities mentioned above can be used for this match. That is, one can use a dynamic piece of discourse such as a natural dialog for the text. Then the more static techniques of illustration, explanation, and demonstration can be used to focus students'

---

[7] James Asher's Total Physical Response method.

attention on the text itself and its cohesion, rather than on pragmatic or semantic factors. Obviously, a great deal of text-based experience and work are necessary to develop a student's skill in this type of match, but the skill is vital for effective writing and, in certain respects, effective reading.

RESOURCES

Each structure-factor match mentioned above suggests resources which can be exploited in making the match clear to students. The structure-social match and the dynamic techniques it suggests in turn suggest teacher activities and student activities, such as roleplaying, storytelling, and student-generated skits; indeed, any resource which allows students to understand and focus on social factors that affect language use would be appropriate. Thus, resources take us one step further toward a concrete lesson plan. Having determined the larger factors that need emphasis and then suitable techniques, the next step is to select material or choose resources.

In addition to the activities mentioned above, there are also resources that consist of objects, such as pictures, realia, and graphics. These can be used for matching structural and semantic factors, since semantic distinctions often need visual reinforcement. For example, the difference between *in the box* and *on the box* can be illustrated by putting something into, then onto a box.

Finally, there are integrated techniques and resources that consist of both a linguistic "object" and a related activity. For example, a song, a verse, or a problem is a text (i.e., a linguistic object), but singing the song, reciting the verse, or solving the problem is a linguistic activity. These resources appear best suited to a structure-discourse match.

Thus, some resources are better than others in helping students make a particular type of match. A roleplay is dynamic and can illustrate socio-linguistic variables. It's a marvelous resource, but probably wasted on teaching locative prepositions. On the other hand, a graphic aid showing three cats in graduated sizes or three stuffed animals would probably illustrate comparatives and superlatives quite well, whereas a roleplay would not be as appropriate in this situation. However,

neither graphics nor roleplay would be an efficient or insightful way
to approach logical connectors such as *even though* or *unless*.

As a review of these points, consider the following grid.

Three Elements to Match with Structure			
	Factors	*Technique*	*Resources*
structure +	social	dynamic interactional techniques (e.g., dramatization)	socially oriented activities (e.g., skits, roleplay)
structure +	semantic	listening and responding; demonstration; illustration; static techniques	objects such as pictures, realia, graphs
structure +	discourse	text generation and manipulation; explanation	linguistic objects and activities such as songs, problems, stories

For each structure, one of the three language-factor matches
can be made. Once that match is made, there are certain techniques
which would be most appropriate to realize the match and certain
resources which would be most helpful in employing that technique.
This matching of structure with language factor, technique, and
resource takes advantage of natural tendencies in language and
pedagogy. In this book, we have tried to indicate these various matches.
While the book is organized around techniques and resources, these
should be construed as tendencies which facilitate explanation and
generalization, not as hard and fast categories or rules.

CONCLUSION

In this chapter we have presented our case for teaching grammar. While
it is not yet conclusive, the evidence available suggests that we proceed with caution in forming judgments about the necessity of grammar instruction. In any case, it is clear that no one should dismiss
grammar instruction altogether, because there is no empirical evidence
that to do so is ultimately more beneficial to second-language learn-

ing. Indeed, some of the alternatives might be harmful in the long run. By forcing learners into communication tasks beyond their grammatical competence, such alternatives may encourage pidginization and premature fossilization.

In this chapter we have also defended an eclectic approach to grammar teaching because of the number and complexity of learner variables. In an effort to improve on traditional methods of teaching grammar, we have proposed a natural matching of structure, language factor, technique, and resources, a procedure which exploits natural divisions in language and pedagogy and thus helps teachers prepare suitable and effective lessons. This matching process will be used throughout the book as a frame of reference for each technique and resource presented and underlies the choice of structures. Because it is the consensus of our colleagues that the communicative phase of a grammar lesson is the most difficult, we have tried to give extra emphasis to this aspect of teaching grammar.

Our techniques are rooted in our experiences in the classroom and those of our colleagues. We present only techniques we feel are workable; however, as we all know, what works for one teacher may not work for another, at least not without considerable modification.

We leave it up to you, the teacher, to amend and adapt these leesons as your creativity, inspiration, and classes dictate. We hope you will enjoy reading this book and be able to use many of our teaching suggestions in your English classes. Even more, we hope our suggestions will encourage you to create your own activities for teaching grammar. After all, you know your students' needs and understand what works best for them.

·ACTIVITIES·

Discussion Questions

1. What approach(es) to second- or foreign-language teaching have you experienced as a learner? Were they rule-based or meaning-and-use-based? How was grammar treated?

2. Based on your experience as a language learner and/or teacher, do you think Higgs and Clifford's characterization of a "terminal 2/2 +" has any merit? Why or why not?

3. Do you think the proposed association of grammar structures with social, semantic, and discourse factors describes natural divisions in language and pedagogy? Why or why not? Would you draw the lines differently? If so, how?

4. Given a particular match between a structure and language factor, do you agree with the authors that certain techniques and resources are natural pedagogical tools? Why or why not?

5. What kind of match applies for teaching the following and why?
— tag questions (Jack's a teacher, *isn't he?*)
— correlatives (*Either* John or Jane will win the contest.)
— indirect speech (Mary said that *Carol was her cousin.*) ·
— attributive adjectives (A *trusted* friend will take care of all the details.)

6. Recall an ESL class you have observed. Was grammar overtly taught? If so, how? Was the lesson effective? How do you know? What elements in the lesson made you consider it effective or ineffective? Would you use the same approach in your classroom? Why or why not?

·CHAPTER TWO·
Basic Issues

GETTING READY TO TEACH GRAMMAR

WHAT IS GRAMMAR?

We can think of language as a type of rule-governed behavior. Grammar, then, is a subset of those rules which govern the configurations that the morphology and syntax of a language assume. These rules are a part of what is "known" automatically by all native speakers of a language; in fact, they do not exist outside of native speakers. That is, there is no English, French, or German which exists independently of its speakers. A language (and by definition, its rules) exists in the individual brains of native speakers. These rules in our brains are usually so automatic and familiar to us as native speakers that we are probably not able to articulate them, but we all certainly know when they are being violated. For example, the rules of English allow us to accept the following sentences as grammatical:

    1. a. He goes to school every day.

        b. Where are you going?

        c. I can't hear you.

However, those same rules force us to reject the following sentences, which contain typical ESL learner errors:

    2. a. *He go to school every day.

        b. *Where you are going?

        c. *I no can hear you.

Of course, it is likely that the sentences in (2) would be understood even though they are ungrammatical; and in some situations, it is undoubtedly better to be able to communicate with sentences like those in (2) than not to be able to communicate at all. However, as we have discussed, in many situations such sentences are simply not sufficient. The communication needs of our students may require that their language conform more closely to the rules of English grammar used by native speakers.

WHAT IS THE RIGHT WAY TO SAY IT?

Usually we have no trouble identifying an ungrammatical sentence. A problem arises, however, when our students want to know "the right way to say it." Much to our mutual dismay, we don't always have a ready answer. For example, consider the following:

3. a. There's two books on the table.
   b. There are two books on the table.
4. a. Going to class now?
   b. Are you going to class now?
5. a. We will talk to you later.
   b. We shall talk to you later.
6. a. Do you have a pencil?
   b. Have you a pencil?

Traditional English grammarians would tell us that (3a) is ungrammatical while (3b) is correct: in sentences with existential *there* the verb agrees with the logical subject of the sentence (*books*), which follows the verb. Because *books* is plural, the verb must be plural. This rather elementary "rule" notwithstanding, sentences such as (3a) routinely occur in the informal conversation of educated speakers of both North American and British English. How do we account for this discrepancy between a prescribed rule in a grammar book and the actual speech of native speakers? Perhaps the following more accurately captures the actual rule followed by native speakers: in informal conversation, *there's* is used with both singular and plural logical subjects, but only in the contracted form. In formal speech or writing, however, (3b) is required. Thus, in this and many other cases, there are different rules for informal speech and formal or written English.

The sentences in (4) illustrate another difference between spoken and written English. In speech we often omit the subject and auxiliary verb in a *yes/no* question, particularly when the subject of the question is the second person (i.e., the person being addressed). In most written English, however, the same omission would be unacceptable, illustrating once again that there are some differences between the rules of written and spoken English.

Of the two sentences in (5), only (5b) is correct according to the old prescriptive rule that states one should use *shall* with the first person subject pronouns *I* and *we*, but *will* with other pronoun subjects, yet (5a) is what most educated native speakers of North American English say. This rule is a prescriptive one that does not accurately describe what most English speakers say or write. Clearly, in some situations, a prescriptive rule that has no basis in usage is not very useful and may even be counter-productive for ESL learners who want to use English the way that native speakers do.

The sentences in example (6) represent the North American and British dialects respectively, but which one is correct? In the United States, (6a) is unquestionably more appropriate, but is (6b) wrong? It is not ungrammatical, and in England (and in the United States many years ago) it is the preferred form for questions in which *have* is the main verb; however, in North America, questions with *have* as the main verb are formed with *do* support, as in (6a).

Even when we are using an approach which does not explicitly teach grammar, it is impossible to avoid such questions from alert and observant ESL students. Often, neither choice is wrong, but one is more or less appropriate, depending on register, communicative purpose, and other pragmatic factors.

LANGUAGE ACADEMIES

For most major languages of the world, it is easy to decide whether a given word, phrase, or sentence is correct or incorrect. The rules governing these languages are promulgated by academies or equivalent national institutions that decide such issues, taking questions of grammar, spelling, writing systems, and coinage of new words, as well as matters of general language policy, out of the hands of the general populace.[1] English-speaking countries, however, have never established language academies. As a result, the rule variations illustrated

---

[1] For a discussion of language academies, see Cooper (in preparation).

above complicate the teaching and learning of English. It is interesting to note that in addition to making English difficult to teach and to learn, the lack of an official academy stimulates as an epiphenomenon the appearance of "pop" grammarians, like John Simon and Edwin Newman. The popularity of these "language guardians" relies crucially on our acceptance of the notion of "absolute correctness." Such a notion is surprisingly popular, even among many of us who should be highly suspicious.

Students who come from countries where language academies prescribe usage often feel there can be only one set of correct rules for English. Since English has no language-academy-set rules, the most realistic approach to determining good usage may be to observe the standard set by educated native speakers in a variety of settings. Linguists have long taken this approach and have provided us with numerous descriptions of what people actually say or write rather than with prescriptions that reflect unrealistic abstractions. If the common goal of ESL teachers and students is communicative competence, the appropriateness of what is said becomes as important as correctness, and appropriateness can only be ascertained by means of a descriptive approach.

Although, as we have noted, language variation in English occurs between speech and writing, between formal and informal usage, between North American and British dialects, and along other dimensions as well, all of these varieties still share enough rules to be considered English. However, we must keep in mind that whenever we are teaching grammar or answering questions about grammar, we are dealing with variable rules. ESL teachers will always have to exercise judgment and common sense in determining what to teach and what to accept.

CORRECTION AND FEEDBACK

Whether an utterance is ungrammatical or not is usually an unambiguous issue. On the other hand, the question of what, when, and how to correct is often problematic. Experience will quickly reveal that it is impossible to correct every error a student makes. Clearly, the ESL/EFL teacher needs to set priorities. One priority is errors in the grammatical structures that are being taught at the moment. These errors should be corrected immediately, as they occur.

For the next priority, we turn to Burt and Kiparsky (1974), who maintain that comprehensibility is the criterion for identifying what needs to be corrected. They suggest that ESL learner errors are hierarchical; that is, some errors make a sentence more difficult to understand than others. They further divide errors into two broad categories, global and local:

> Global mistakes are those that violate rules involving the overall structure of a sentence, the relations among constituent clauses or, in a simple sentence, the relations among major constituents. Local mistakes cause touble in a particular constituent or in a clause of a complex sentence. (p. 73)

For Burt and Kiparsky, global errors are higher in the hierarchy than local ones. This suggests that errors involving word order, missing obligatory constituents such as subjects, and misuse of semantically full connectors or those that confuse the relationship of clauses or sentential constituents are more important than an omitted article or inflectional morpheme in the third person singular. For example, let us consider the student-generated sentence (7a) below. Burt and Kiparsky point out that correcting the global error of word order (7b) facilitates understanding to a greater degree than correcting two local errors of subject-verb agreement and an omitted article in (7c).

7. a. English language use much people.
   b. Much people use English language.
   c. The English language uses many people.

Burt and Kiparsky also claim that it is easier for a student to recognize and correct a global error than a local one. This is certainly true for native speakers of English, as Tomiyama (1980) has demonstrated. On the other hand, research by Master (1986) suggests that with proper systematic instruction and focus on form, the frequency of even the most recalcitrant of local errors can be reduced significantly.

Although our experience, for the most part, is consistent with Burt and Kiparsky's observations and conclusions, there are certain situations in which local errors affect the comprehensibility of a sentence as much as global errors. We are thinking of local cases such as quantifiers and the distinction between gerunds and infinitives. For example, in (8a) below, John does have some good ideas, whereas (8b) is an insult.

8. a. John has a few good ideas.
   b. John has few good ideas.

In (9a), John didn't pay the rent. In (9b), he paid the rent, but forgot he had done so.

9. a. John forgot to pay the rent.
   b. John forgot paying the rent.

ESL students often substitute (8b) for (8a) or (9a) for (9b), and such local errors can and do affect comprehensibility.

Last, but certainly not least, is any error that stigmatizes the user or identifies him as a member of a group to which he might not want to belong. For example, the use of *he don't* or *ain't* might be a stigmatizing error in American English. We suggest that errors that stigmatize the learner should be pointed out immediately, regardless of whether they are the object of pedagogical attention, are global or local, or affect the comprehensibility of the sentence.

We suggest, then, the following priorities for correcting errors:

1. errors which stigmatize the learner
2. errors which are the object of pedagogical attention
3. global errors which affect comprehensibility
4. local errors which affect comprehensibility
5. global and local errors which do not affect comprehensibility

We will have a bit more to say about correction later in this chapter when we discuss those activities in which correction is counter-productive.

SEQUENCING

In addition to deciding which structures to teach and which errors to correct, there is the question of what to teach first. General educational principles suggest we start with the simple and move toward the difficult, but structures that seem, *prima facie*, uncomplicated may in fact be quite difficult for some students to internalize. For example, there is evidence that inflection for the third person singular in the present tense is "late acquired." In other words, most adult learners still omit the obligatory -*s* from third person singular verbs in the present tense long after they have mastered "more complicated" verb forms. Obviously, "simple" and "complex" are meaningless terms if they are not defined from the learner's point of view. Although there have been some attempts to identify a "difficulty" or "acquisition" order in English,[2] the resulting sequences usually deal only with elementary structures and cannot possibly account for every structure in the language. Also, these lists have been created from a structuralist perspective, which may be inadequate and inappropriate if acquisition does not proceed in terms of grammatical structure but according to some other schema.

In describing a natural acquisition order determined by observing children learning German as their L-1, Pienemann (1984) presents convincing evidence that children learning German as a second language do not learn structures for which they are not "ready" (e.g., a structure which is not "next" in the natural acquisition order), even when these structures are overtly taught. One could thus argue that the children who learned the structure were "taught" nothing, were simply ready to take the next step in acquisition, and would have done so regardless of the lessons. Similarly, those who were not ready did not learn. As interesting as these conclusions are, however, we must remember that they apply to children, and, as mentioned earlier, there is a great deal of evidence that child language learning is quite different from adult language learning. Adults learning English do not necessarily go through the same stages of acquisition as children learning English as an L-1, and there is no reason we should expect them to. Thus, sequencing ESL lessons to match the child acquisition order may be needless for children and irrelevant for adults.

An argument could be made for teaching the language of basic social skills early on, such as greetings, holding one's place in a conversation, leave taking, and asking a native speaker for assistance ("How do you say this in English?"). Such an approach would certainly give adult learners a grasp of conversational English very quickly, but might encourage conversation "prematurely" if the hypotheses regarding pidginization and fossilization turn out to be true. (See Chapter 1).

---

[2] See Dulay and Burt (1974); Bailey, Madden, and Krashen (1974); Larsen-Freeman (1975, 1976); Anderson (1978); among others.

Again, in the absence of evidence to the contrary, we are inclined to be conservative and follow the traditional structuralist syllabus, which sequences structures so they "build" on each other. For example, the simple present of the verb *to be* is taught before the present continuous, which requires the conjugated form of *be*, namely *is*, *am*, and *are* and a present participle (verb + *ing*). Despite this inclination, the bottom line regarding sequencing is simply that the issues are exceedingly complex and far from resolved in the current literature.

Few of us have the luxury (or perhaps we should say the burden) of sequencing an ESL program from beginning to end. We are more often obliged to teach district- or school-prescribed syllabuses, which usually are structually based, so let us imagine for the sake of illustration that we are beginning teachers, required to teach the passive voice, in addition to other structures, to our intermediate adult-school class as part of a ten-week semester. Let's follow the lesson from beginning to end.

PREPARATION FOR THE GRAMMAR LESSON

The first step in preparing a grammar lesson is to consult a variety of grammar reference books and ESL texts in order to establish how a structure is formed, when it is used, and whether there are any particular rules or exceptions governing its use. For example, in her English grammar reference, Frank (1972) says of the passive:

> The active voice is used in making a straightforward statement about an action . . . In the passive voice, the same action is referred to indirectly; that is, the original "receiver" of the action is the grammatical subject and the original "doer" of the action is the grammatical object of the preposition *by*. Because the grammatical subject of a passive verb is the original object of an active verb, *only a transitive verb may be used in the passive voice.* (p. 56)

Frank lists the situations in which the passive voice would be chosen over the active voice, including:

1. when attention is being drawn to the "receiver" rather than the "doer" of the action (e.g., *My dog was hit by a car*), and

2. when the "doer" of the action is unimportant or not known. Another point Frank makes is that *get* or *become* can be used instead of *be* as a passive of transition (e.g., *They're getting married tomorrow*).

In another source, Leech and Svartvik (1975) describe the passive as "the type of verb phrase which contains the construction *be* + past participle: *was killed, was seen,* etc." (p. 257). The authors go beyond Frank in saying that not all verbs taking objects have a passive, such as *have* in *I have a Fiat* (but not *A Fiat is had by me*) and *hold* in *This jug holds two pints* (but not *Two pints is held by this jug*). Leech and Svartvik say the agent in the *by*-phrase is retained only in specific cases; in fact, about four out of five English passive clauses do not have an agent. Despite this information, the authors do not enumerate the cases in which the agent is required. They do deal with the *get* passive, but characterize it as belonging to "informal style and in constructions without an agent" (p. 259). However, the following examples come to mind in response to their claim that the *get* passive doesn't normally take an agent: *Tom got hit by a truck,* and *Maurice gets stung by a bee every single summer.* In American English, it seems, *get* passives can retain the agent.

Azar, in her grammar book (1981), mentions that only transitive verbs are used in the passive and that usually the *by*-phrase is omitted, since the agent is generally understood. She also says that the passive ranges over all tenses and she gives the form for the present, past, future, progressive perfect, and simple tenses.

Additional aspects of the passive are given by Celce-Murcia and Larsen-Freeman (1983); they disagree with Frank's claim that the passive is the same action as the active referred to indirectly. As proof, they cite the famous example from Chomsky (1965) which shows that active and passive pairs are not necessarily synonymous: *Everyone in the room speaks two languages* (i.e., any two languages per person) and *Two languages are spoken by everyone in the room* (i.e., two specific languages that everybody speaks). To this we would add an example given to us by Ed Keenan: *Every politician kissed a baby* (i.e., different politicians kissed different babies) and *A baby was kissed by every politician* (i.e., every politician kissed one specific baby).

Celce-Murcia and Larsen-Freeman also counter Azar's claim

that only transitive verbs take a passive with examples that show there
are some passives which do not have active transitive counterparts:
Mehdi was born in Teheran (but not *Someone bore Mehdi in Teheran*)
and *It is rumored that he will get the job* (but not *Someone rumored that
he will get the job*). Thus, they conclude that whether a verb is compatible with the active voice, the passive voice, or both is a property
of the verb.

Another aspect noted by Celce-Murcia and Larsen-Freeman
is that most passives do not have an agent. They cite a usage study
conducted by Shintani which suggests that since 85 percent of all
passives will not retain an agent, we should teach our students when
and why to retain an agent in a passive, rather than teach when to omit
an agent.[3] Shintani's study (1979) includes a list of those situations
in which a *by*-phrase is retained:

1. when the agent is a proper name designating an artist, in-
   ventor, discoverer, innovator, etc., who is too important to
   omit in the context (e.g., *The Mona Lisa was painted by da
   Vinci.*)
2. when the agent is an indefinite noun phrase (i.e., new information) and is retained to provide the listener or reader with
   the new information (i.e., *While Jill was walking down the
   street, her purse was snatched by a young man.*)
3. when the agent is an inanimate noun phrase which is retained
   because it is unexpected . . . (we usually expect an agent to
   be animate, e.g., *All the lights and appliances in the Albertson
   household are switched on and off daily by an electrical device.*)

Celce-Murcia and Larsen-Freeman also mention different kinds of
passives. In addition to the *get* passives already mentioned, they introduce a complex passive with *have*: *Alice had her purse snatched while
shopping downtown.* They explain the differences in meaning among
a simple passive, the *get* passive, and the complex passive with *have*,
as well as stative passives in which the participles function more like
predicate adjectives than passive verbs.

Finally, Celce-Murcia and Larsen-Freeman talk about the circumstances under which the passive is used. Besides the two situa-

---

[3] Celce-Murcia and Larsen-Freeman (1983: 225).

tions provided by Frank, these include:
1. when the agent is obvious and, therefore, not expressed (e.g., *Grapes are grown in the Napa Valley.*)
2. when the writer wants to sound objective (e.g., *It is assumed/ believed that this was among the most significant policy decisions of the decade.*)
3. when the writer wishes to retain the same grammatical subject in successive clauses (e.g., *Rene Arredondo beat Lonnie Smith, but he was beaten by Gato Garcia.*)
4. when the theme is shared information, but the agent is new (e.g., *What a beautiful picture! Isn't it? It was painted by one of my students.*)

Having looked at just two grammar references, one ESL text, and one TESL training text, we already see problems. All of the texts provide interesting and helpful information. However, none is 100 percent complete. Therefore, it is necessary to consult more than one text when preparing to teach a grammar point for the first time. Since not all of the sources will agree, and not all will agree with what we have learned through our own experiences, questions which arise during preparation need to be resolved to some degree before the lesson is presented, since some bright and articulate student will probably notice a discrepancy and ask about it. With this information in mind, let us now plan our strategy for teaching the passive.

The first step is to decide which language factor occurs most naturally with the passive. This structure does not seem particularly sensitive to socio-linguistic factors; whether one uses passive or active does not vary according to whom one is talking to (*Harold was struck by lightning* would not necessarily change to *Lightning struck Harold* as a result of whom one was addressing). Likewise, the semantic content of many (but certainly not all) active/passive pairs is similar, so approaching the passive voice from a semantic perspective would not be very helpful. By the process of elimination, then, we conclude that the most natural match seems to be structure with discourse. With some experience in matching, the process becomes much less arbitrary, and it will be easier to see which language factor most naturally complements a particular structure. Now that we have decided that the passive voice is discourse-sensitive, we will have to provide sufficient discourse context to give a realistic picture of the structure. The techniques which this combination suggests include storytelling, singing, and problem solving. Our resources will be linguistic objects or texts such as stories, songs, dialogs, and verse, combined with appropriate activities.

The second step is to delimit the information so that what we teach matches the ability of our students. In our hypothetical program, this is the first time the class will be learning the passive voice, so we will not include all of the variations, such as *get* passives, complex passives with *have*, and stative passives at this time. Instead we will confine our instruction to the simple *be* passive. Depending on the students' level, we may also limit our focus to one or two tenses.

THE GRAMMAR LESSON

The second step or stage is the grammar lesson, which consists of four parts:

1. **Presentation,** in which we introduce the grammar structure, either inductively or deductively. There are a variety of techniques and resources that can be used during this step. Selection should be made according to teacher strengths, student preferences, and the nature of the structure (e.g., What is the structure-language-factor match?)

2. **Focused practice**, in which the learner manipulates the structure in question while all other variables are held constant. The purpose of this step is to allow the learner to gain control of the form without the added pressure and distraction of trying to use the form for communication. The teacher should not proceed to the next phase until most students have mastered at least the form of the structure.

3. **Communicative practice**, in which the learner engages in communicative activities to practice the structure being learned. According to Morrow and Johnson (1981), a communicative task incorporates the actual processes of communication; the more of these features an exercise incorporates, the more communicative it is.
   - *Information gap.* In the course of doing the activity, one participant should be in a position to tell one or more other people

something that the others do not yet know.

- *Choice*. The speaker must have some role in deciding exactly what he will say and how he will say it. (Options can be presented in advance by the teacher.) This also means that there should be some uncertainty in the mind of the listener(s) about what the speaker will say next.
- *Feedback*. What the speaker says to the person(s) he is communicating with depends not only on what the other person(s) says, but also on what the speaker wants to accomplish via the conversation (pp. 62–63).

4. **Teacher feedback and correction**. Although this is usually considered a final step, it must take place throughout the lesson. We also feel that a teacher's correction strategy should probably change according to the phase of the lesson. For example, during the second part of the lesson, correction should be predominantly straightforward and immediate. During the third part, however, communication should not be interrupted. Instead, the teacher should take note of errors and deal with them after the communicative exercises. There is one element of correction, however, that we feel should remain constant; regardless of when correction is made, teacher feedback should always attempt to engage the student cognitively rather than to simply point out the error and provide the appropriate target form. In any case, the match in language factors, technique, and resources will be used in each part of the lesson.

For additional discussion of each phase, see Chapter Ten, which includes a remedial minigrammar lesson. The differences between the abbreviated version of a grammar lesson described there and a regular lesson are the length of each phase, the variety in the presentation, and the remedial nature of the minigrammar lesson. The minilesson assumes that the structure has been taught, but for some reason has ceased to be an active part of the repertoire of at least some of the students. A regular grammar lesson is much more substantial and generally presents a grammar concept for the first time.

Because review is essential in our program (like many adult schools, our imaginary school has a policy of open enrollment, so that students may enter our class at any time during the semester), we will teach the passive voice after reviewing the major tenses and aspects.

As we cycle through each tense to review over the next few weeks, we will include the passive voice for that particular tense and aspect. In other words, we will introduce the passive in present and past tense now, but when we review the present perfect some weeks hence, we will introduce the passive voice of the present perfect. In this way, we will be able to cover the passive voice with various verb tenses and aspects once the basic concept has been understood and mastered, and we will not have to give students so much initial data that they lose sight of the general picture.

Since we have established that the active and passive versions of a sentence are not always as closely tied as we had first imagined, we will not teach passive sentences by simply transforming active ones. We will teach the passive in its own right, not as a structure derived from an active sentence. We will start out by teaching the passive *without* the agent *by*-phrase because naming the agent through a *by*-phrase is unusual—not commonplace—in the passive voice. Only later will we teach the exceptions that allow students to retain the agent.

Finally, for this lesson we should keep in mind that not all passives have an active, transitive counterpart, and we will therefore teach "passivization" as a property of the verb (i.e., some verbs can be used in passive sentences and some cannot; whether a given verb can or not is not a function of transitivity, but rather a property of the verb, although, of course, there is a strong correlation between verbs that are transivitive and verbs that passivize).

Now that we have made the basic preliminary decisions, we will describe an actual lesson we observed in an adult school in terms of the steps outlined above. We visited the class of an experienced teacher who had excellent rapport with her class, which consisted of fifty-one students, predominantly from Latin America, about evenly divided between male and female. The teacher was comfortable with the number of students, as well as with the subject matter and the techniques used. The techniques were appropriate for the structure she was teaching and worked well for her, but they are not necessarily appropriate for everyone. It is important for each of us to explore and develop techniques which are compatible with our personalities and philosophies. Recall that we have suggested that any grammar lesson has four parts: (1) presentation, (2) structured, focused practice, (3) communicative practice, and (4) feedback and correction. We will begin by describing the observed teacher's presentation.

Presentation

The teacher's first objective was to focus students' attention on the structure in a natural context for the passive. Her second aim in the presentation phase was to elicit the rule for forming the passive from the students rather than simply telling them the rule. Her technique was a roleplay/storytelling combination. She began by selecting a student from the class and having her come to the front of the room with her purse. She whispered to the student briefly, explaining what was going to happen so that the student would not be startled or upset. She then selected another student to play the role of a thief. She directed the second student to run by the first student, grab her purse, and run to the back of the room. The teacher assured us that most students love a roleplay, and that she had never seen students take this one seriously or become upset or agitated by it. We would caution, however, that if you think the students you are working with would not respond well to this situation, you might want to select another context in which the focus will naturally be on the one who receives rather than the one who performs the action, such as being invited to the movies by a famous person.

  The teacher felt that by the time students reach an intermediate level, they should be proficient at both hamming it up and participating as an audience. Her narration of the scene for the class follows:

  "You know, last night Luisa was walking home from her friend's house when suddenly something terrible happened."

At this point, the second student was cued to run by and steal the purse.

  "Her purse was stolen! Oh my goodness! That was terrible! Luisa, what happened?"

The teacher then allowed Luisa to enjoy her role by giving the class as much detail about the incident as she wanted, and involved the other students as much as they wanted. As soon as everything settled down, the teacher helped Luisa to her seat and said:

  "You poor thing! That's too bad! Here, let me help you to your seat."

Then the teacher said to the class:

"Wasn't that awful? Luisa is going to call the police right away, and what is she going to tell them?"

Then the teacher elicited answers from the class and wrote on the board,

My purse was stolen.

She then shifted the class's attention to the student at the back of the room with the purse, who had been forgotten in all the excitement. Her narration continued:

"Well, here's the thief. Carmen. Let's see what happened to her. She was chased all over the city by the police."

The teacher acted as both narrator and police officer, chasing Carmen around the room and giving commentary on the action in the passive voice. After everyone had enjoyed the action, the teacher shouted, "Halt!" and then continued:

"Finally Carmen was caught. She was frisked and then she was handcuffed, and finally she was taken to jail. And what happened to Luisa's purse? It was given back to her."

The teacher returned Luisa's purse, thanked the students for participating, and asked everyone to be seated. Returning to the chalkboard, she said:

"Now, what happened to Carmen?"

She wrote each statement on the board after eliciting it from a student. Not all of the suggestions were grammatically correct, but when students couldn't provide the form exactly, the teacher accepted appropriate content and put the grammatically correct form on the board in order to give feedback:

She was chased, she was caught . . .

After all the forms were written on the board, the teacher proceeded as follows:

"Now this is sort of interesting. We have a new grammatical form here. Does anyone know what this is called?"

No student could provide the name of the form, so she said:

"This is called the passive voice."

Then she explained why the context demanded use of the passive voice. Her explanation was more like a dialog with the students than a lecture. It went something like this:

"What is important to Luisa?"

The students responded, "Her purse."

"That's right. Luisa is interested in her purse. She doesn't even know the person who took it. The thief isn't interesting. If Luisa calls you on the phone to tell you about her experience, what are you interested in?"

Again, the students responded, "Her purse."

"That's right. And that's why Luisa is talking about her purse, not the person who took it. Sometimes we're more interested in what receives the action than what does the action. In this case, the person who did the action is a stranger. We're not interested in her. We want to talk about what's important to us. So this is one time we would use the passive voice in English."

She then wrote the rule on the board, under the heading *Passive Voice*.

The next focus of attention was form. Referring to the sentences she had written on the board, the teacher asked:

"Can you see what the pattern is? How do we make the passive voice?"

She worked with the students until the correct rule of *be* + past participle was arrived at. Technically, the passive is formed with a passive participle, but for all intents and purposes, it is identical to the past participle, so the teacher used the term "past participle" to draw on what her students already knew. At this point, she then reviewed exactly what the forms of the verb *be* are, writing each on the board:

"Now what is the verb *be* again? *Am, are, is, was,* and *were,* and when do I use *am*? *Are*?" (etc.)

She put the pronouns by the verb so that she finally had the paradigm, *I am, you are, he/she/it is,* etc. on the board, and then reviewed past participles as the "third part of the verb" and went through several verbs, writing the base form, simple past, and past participle on the board. After this minireview, she turned to the passive sentences her students had formed about the scene their classmates had performed and pointed out and underlined the verb *be* and the past participle in each example, as well as the rule for its production that had been elicited from the class. She then erased the sentences about Luisa and the fate of the thief and called a young man to the front of the class.

"Everyone knows Ali. Ali, say hello to everyone."

Ali hammed it up.

"You know, a few months ago, Ali did something very wonderful. He helped a lot of poor people in this city, which was a very
fine and important thing to do. In fact, it was so wonderful that
the mayor held a special ceremony for Ali last week. Did you
know that? Ali, is it true?"
Once again, Ali did his part.
"Let me tell you what happened at that ceremony. Ali was given
. . . what's this called?"
Someone supplied the term *a medal*. The teacher pinned a paper medal
she had made on Ali's chest and asked:
"What happened to Ali? Everyone write it down on your paper,
but don't say it. Give everyone a chance to get it."
She waited a few minutes and then asked the class:
"What happened to Ali?"
A student volunteered the answer, "Ali was given a medal," and the
teacher wrote it on the board, repeating it as she wrote. She then went
over each element of the sentence and asked:
"How many people got this right?"
Several students raised their hands. She acknowledged them and then
continued with Ali's story, using the same procedure for each main
point:
"And he was congratulated by a lot of important people. His
picture was taken,"
Here the teacher again simulated the action and had the students try
to write on their papers before she provided the narration for the event:
"and he was given the key to the city."
The teacher presented a "key," with a brief side discussion about what
it meant to receive the key to the city. At each step the teacher asked
for a show of hands of how many students had gotten the sentence
correct. She told us she was using this as an informal evaluation process, and she would continue the story of Ali or begin a new story until
about 80 percent of the class was correctly producing the passive on
their papers. As an additional verification, she walked around the room
as she told the story, informally checking papers during the pauses
when students were writing. When she was satisfied, she addressed
the class, standing by a very proud Ali,
"Don't you feel proud just to know him? Let's give him a hand."

All the students applauded. The teacher then returned to the line of reasoning begun before.

> "Now, what are we interested in, the person who gave Ali the medal or our friend, Ali? What's more interesting to us, the person who took his picture or Ali?"

At each point the students responded properly and the teacher said:

> "That's right, and that's why we say . . ."

She again reviewed the context for the passive and the rule for constructing it, and then she moved into the second phase of the lesson.

Focused Practice

Recall that in this part of a grammar lesson students are asked simply to manipulate the structure under consideration. To accomplish this task, the teacher asked the students to imagine they were writing home about their classmate, Ali, and his award ceremony. She put these sentences on the board and asked students to fill in the appropriate form of the verb.

Dear _____ ,

Last night an award ceremony ____(1)____ for my friend, Ali. He
                              (hold)
is a real hero in this city, and last night he ____(2)____ a medal
                                                  (give)
for his bravery. Everyone ____(3)____ . After the ceremony, his
                            (impress)
picture ____(4)____ with the mayor and everyone wanted his auto-
          (take)
graph. Later there was a party at a fancy restaurant to celebrate. We

all ____(5)____ . It was fantastic! We danced and drank champagne
      (invite)
until two in the morning. Truly, a good time ____(6)____ by all. I'll
                                               (have)
write more later. Bye for now.

Love,

_____

Students copied the letter from the board and filled in the blanks with the passive form (*was* or *were* and the past participle of the verb in parentheses). As students were working, the teacher walked around the room, answered questions, and worked individually with students who were having trouble or who asked for help.

When everyone had finished, the teacher selected a volunteer to fill in the blanks on the board. Members of the class then took turns reading aloud from the board. The teacher corrected any errors immediately with the help of students. Finally, she asked students to check their work against the examples on the board. During this phase of the lesson, the teacher gave careful attention to correction. She was circulating in the room, correcting errors as she found them. Her last step was to ask how many students had gotten all the answers correct, only one wrong, only two wrong, etc. As students raised their hands, she looked around and acknowledged each.

This concluded her presentation and focused practice of the passive. Her lesson lasted about thirty-five minutes. Each day for about one and a half weeks she planned to review the previous day's work and introduce a new context and some structured practice for the passive voice.

Communicative Practice

The teacher didn't really give the class any communicative exercises (the third phase of a grammar lesson) until about a week after introducing the passive, when she was confident that most students could at least manipulate the form and use it in a controlled context. For her first communicative activity, the class was divided into pairs. One member of each pair was sent to an adjoining room, and the door was closed so they could not see what was going to happen. Then an aide, Alan, whose help had been solicited before class, came to the front of the room. The students laughed while a silly hat was put on Alan, a mustache was drawn, a fingernail was painted green, etc. While the victim retreated to clean himself up, the second members of the pairs were called back to the room. The teacher explained that students who had stayed in the room had to tell their partners what had happened to Alan, using the passive voice. During the communicative exercises, no corrections were made, but the teacher circulated around the room, noting errors in her notebook.

Feedback and Correction

The next day's grammar lesson began with the teacher writing several errors she had overheard the day before on the board. She said to the class, "Yesterday during our lesson I heard someone say this. What do you think about this sentence?" She then elicited the correct form from the class and did a very quick focused review, much like the structured, focused exercises mentioned in our description of the presentation phase of the lesson. Next she moved into another communicative exercise and alternated between phases two and three until she was satisfied with her students' mastery of the structure.

Lesson Summary

Because we have decided the most frequent and natural context for the passive voice is written discourse (Shintani, Quirk, *et al.* 1985), more advanced or sophisticated students might respond better or more comfortably to some of the exercises for the passive that appear in Chapter Eleven. We have explained what we observed one adult-school teacher do successfully, but of course presentation, focused practice, communicative practice, and correction and feedback procedures will vary according to the natural inclinations and preferences of the teacher and students.

In addition to the lesson we saw and the teacher's projected lessons, we would suggest a lesson toward the end of the unit illustrating when the agent *by*-phrase is retained in a passive sentence and another one on verbs that occur only in the passive (e.g., *to be born*).

CONCLUSION

In this chapter we began by considering what language really is and the difference between prescriptive and descriptive grammar, so we could more rationally evaluate material in preparation for a grammar lesson. We parenthetically considered the issue of sequencing and then began to prepare for the lesson much in the same way any ESL teacher would prepare to teach a grammar point for the first time.

We looked up the passive in two reference texts, an ESL text, and a TESL text. We noticed similarities and differences among the texts and compared them to our own experience and common sense.

Then we summarized our findings. Our next step was to determine the match between structure, language factors, techniques, and resources so that we could select appropriate techniques and resources for the lesson.

Finally, we described in detail an actual thirty-five minute grammar lesson for teaching the passive voice and the sequencing the teacher planned to follow over a period of time as she moved through the four phases of teaching grammar:

- presentation
- focused practice
- communicative practice
- feedback and correction

·ACTIVITIES·

Discussion Questions

1. Why is it so difficult to give hard and fast rules for English grammar?

2. This chapter suggests that a grammar lesson might optimally consist of four phases. What reasoning do you think motivated these divisions? Do you agree or disagree? Justify your position.

3. Based on your experience as a language learner and/or teacher, do you agree with the suggestions in the grammar lesson regarding correction and feedback? Why or why not?

4. What did you think of the grammar lesson presented in this chapter? How would you change the lesson to make it work for you and your students?

Suggested Activities

1. Select a grammar point. Look it up in a grammar reference book, a text for ESL students, and a reference text for ESL teachers. Do the three agree with each other? On what points do they disagree?

2. Plan a grammar lesson on the point you researched in the previous question. List in detail the steps you decide to incorporate into your grammar lesson.

·CHAPTER THREE·
Techniques

LISTENING AND RESPONDING

Let us begin our discussion of techniques by considering one which is particularly well suited to both presentation and focused practice of grammar structures with a semantic challenge: the technique of listening and responding.

Most of us, at one time or another, have seen young children learning a second language. In contrast to adults, most children seem to learn second and third languages almost effortlessly. For example, the children of adult immigrants are almost always considerably more proficient in their second language than their elders and, unlike their parents, they often achieve native-like fluency and pronunciation. No one is absolutely certain why this occurs, but one of the *prima facie* differences in language acquisition between adults and children is that the children observe a "silent period." According to researchers, children often don't say anything or say very little when first learning a second language. They appear simply to listen; then, after a while, the new language begins to emerge naturally.

Many methodologists feel that adult second-language learners, like children learning their first language, should be allowed to enjoy a silent period and that if we didn't force our adult learners to speak and repeat phrases in the new language immediately, adults would be much better language learners. Moreover, from our reading of Blair (1983), we know that not all adults are poor second-language learners. Blair cites work done by Hill (1970), who reports on Indians living in the Amazon basin, among whom "the learning of new languages in both childhood and adulthood is widespread and thought to be perfectly ordinary" (p. 240). Approximately twenty-four distinct

languages are spoken in this area, and the culture of these peoples
demands that they marry someone from another language group. To
do otherwise is considered incestuous. Thus, children are minimally
bilingual before they reach adolescence, speaking the native languages
of both parents, and often learn several more languages in adulthood.
Of particular relevance to our discussion on listening is how the Indians
learn these different languages:

> The Indians do not practice speaking a language that they do
> not know well yet. Instead, they passively learn lists of words,
> forms, and phrases in it and familiarize themselves with the
> sound of its pronunciation. . . . They may make an occasional
> attempt to speak . . . in an appropriate situation, but if it does
> not come easily, they will not force it.[1]

Blair also cites Nida (1971), who reports that many African polyglots
have told him that after listening to a language long enough, they can
"hear" it. One African said, "We just live there and listen, and before
we know it, we can hear what they say. Then we can talk" (p. 42).

While conducting research at the Defense Language Institute
in Monterey, California, Postovsky (1970, 1975, 1976) found that,
among students of Russian, the development of comprehension skills
significantly facilitated the acquisition of speaking skills. Postovsky
speculated that comprehension constituted a latency from which speech
production would emerge naturally. Likewise, TPR—in which the first
weeks or months of a student's second language learning consist of
physically responding to a series of oral commands in the target
language—has been an effective approach for both younger and older
second-language learners, particularly at the beginning levels (Asher,
1965 and Asher et al., 1974).[2]

Not all students are willing or able to observe a silent period.
Cultural expectations or practical obligations may force them to interact verbally; they need to ride the bus, hold down a job or go to school,
pay the rent, enroll children in school, etc. It may thus be unrealistic
to enforce a strict silent period with adolescent or adult ESL learners;

---

[1] Sorenson (1967: 680), cited in Hill.
[2] For a discussion of this method and an example lesson using TPR, see Larsen-
Freeman (1986).

however, it appears that some kind of compromise that includes work on listening comprehension for part of the time is more beneficial than the standard "listen and repeat" classes we see in many schools.

Banjar (1981) conducted an experiment involving just this kind of compromise in Saudi Arabian secondary schools. Four classes, each with four hours of English per week, participated in the experiment. Two experimental classes devoted the first fifteen minutes of each lesson to listening comprehension using *The Learnables*, materials developed by Harris Winitz. The materials consist of picture books (no written text) accompanied by tapes recorded by native speakers. The tapes describe the pictures in sequence, and students simply listen and turn the pages. The two control classes in Banjar's experiment did other activities irrelevant to the experimental treatment during the first fifteen minutes of each lesson. Both groups were tested at the beginning and the end of the experiment. After three months, "Students in the experimental group who received the listening component performed significantly better . . . not only on listening comprehension but also on other language skills such as grammar and dictation" (Banjar 1981: 32).

A very good way of achieving the kind of compromise Banjar's research supports is for the language teacher to speak only the target language, in class and out. It is natural for teachers to want to demonstrate their mastery of the students' native language, or to want native speakers with whom they can practice a language they are learning. However, when language teachers use their students for either of these purposes, they do so at the expense of the students. Conversation with students outside of class on routine matters may be the only opportunity to converse about personal or real-life situations in the target language. We know some teachers who will allow students to address them in either their native or the target language, but these teachers will respond only in the target language. In this way, if students have personal messages or problems that they cannot express in the target language, they can still communicate with the teacher yet they also receive target language input. Moreover, students who may constitute a language minority in a class will very likely feel left out and rejected if the teacher addresses everyone in the class (except them) in a language to which they are not privy. Besides being extraordinarily rude, such behavior suggests an intimacy and understanding with some of the students from which the others are excluded. Affective factors are exceedingly important in second-language acquisition, and to be excluded by one's language teacher, whether the rejection is real or imagined, intentional or unintentional, can be devastating.

We have had colleagues who argue energetically and even persuasively for the expediency of offering a word now and then in the native language of the students if the class has one common language; however, we must admit that we remain unconvinced. Our experience as second- and third-language learners and as second-language teachers suggests to us that the safest and most satisfying policy in the long run is for us to speak the target language at all times with our students, and this is our advice to you. It may take more time to explain a vocabulary item in the target language, and you may need to make several attempts, but each attempt constitutes listening comprehension practice of authentic language used for communicative purposes and should thus ultimately be beneficial to the students, even if it does not instantly achieve the immediate goal.

The exercises in this chapter are based on the assumption that listening comprehension is necessary for second-language acquisition. They encourage learners to make a match between structure and meaning while observing a silent period and are thus ideally suited to beginning students. More experienced students can also benefit from this approach because it will help them to comprehend a structure before they are asked to produce it. For structures that have a semantic association, the listening exercises in this chapter can be used as the basis for activities in which students are asked to listen and respond, physically or verbally. The resources needed for this technique are objects and people, mainly the students themselves.

LISTEN AND PHYSICALLY RESPOND

Our first exercise, which draws on Asher's Total Physical Response method (1977), is a very effective way to present imperatives, prepositions, and phrasal verbs. Although it is a presentation technique for students at all levels, it can also provide structured and communicative practice for beginning students who don't have enough language to handle a communicative task. Asher's research suggests that students benefit from watching as well as from doing, so you can begin by bringing several students and their chairs to the front of the room. The rest of the class will watch and learn. Have students sit down and face the class. Be careful not to use any language except English. Say "Stand up," and do it yourself to show your students what you mean. Do it several times until the students in the front of the room get the idea. Then ask individual students to do it. Use their names: "John, stand up." When John does it correctly, acknowledge this by saying, "good" or "OK." After all the students in the front of the room can do it, try a new command: "Mary, sit down." Go slowly. Repeat and act out each command as many times as necessary. When students can stand up or sit down on command, ask one to walk to the window. Remember, you can demonstrate yourself or use gestures, but don't answer any questions in the student's native language. Everything must be in English. Continue with other directions, such as, "Stand up," "Sit down," "Jump," "Walk to the window," and "Walk to the chair." When they have mastered these commands, you can give them a novel command they haven't heard before, such as, "Jump to the window." Students will be delighted when they realize they can understand and respond to something new in English in so short a time. In this way, students learn to comprehend the imperative form without even realizing it.

LISTEN AND DRAW

For working with students beyond the very beginning level, the following activity might be used for communicative practice of prepositions and locations of objects with various shapes.

Ask students to take out a piece of paper and a pencil. Tell them to listen and to draw what you ask. You can make the directions as simple or complex as you want. The following example starts out very simply, but becomes quite complex:

"Draw a heart in the upper right-hand corner of your paper. Now draw a diamond to the left of the heart. Draw a house in the middle of your paper. Now draw a tree three inches below the heart. Put two horizontal, parallel lines three centimeters below the diamond."

This exercise can continue as long as your students are challenged and can be varied to practice vocabulary and prepositions receptively.

LISTEN AND COLOR

For receptive practice of possessive adjectives, the following activity can be used. Give students some crayons and a mimeographed sheet with line drawings of a boy and a girl, and their dogs. The pictures can be simple, but students must be able to tell the boy from the girl. Then give the class the following instructions:

> "On your paper there are two people, a boy and a girl. Color his hair red."

Wait for students to do this, and then say:

> "Color her hair orange. Color her skirt brown. Color his pants black. Color her T-shirt green. Color his T-shirt purple. Color his dog brown and white. Color her dog yellow."

The actual colors used are not important. The main objective is to give students a chance to follow directions while listening to colors and possessive adjectives in imperative sentences. When the students are finished, let them compare papers. Finally, show them your paper as a final check for accuracy. This activity is intended for children, but adults enjoy it or adaptations of it as well. If you cannot prepare mimeographed sheets for your students, you can draw the pictures on the board and have students approximate them on paper; two students can also come up to the front of the room and carry out the commands with colored chalk. The rest of the students can watch and correct their classmates if a mistake is made.

LISTEN AND MANIPULATE

A particularly effective technique for presenting or practicing prepositions and phrasal verbs requires your students to listen and manipulate objects. If you are using the following exercise to present the lesson, follow the TPR format outlined on page 43, in which the teacher demonstates the appropriate action first.

> For example, call one student to the front of the room and say: "John, put the book on the table. Good. Put the book under the table. Good. Put the book beside the chair. Good. Put the book in the drawer."

Introduce the phrasal verb *pick up* by continuing this way:

> "Pick up the book and put it on the chair. Pick up the book and put it in the drawer."

For more advanced students who have mastered prepositions of location, you can extend the activity to demonstrate other uses of prepositions, such as the proxy function of *for*. To do this, say:

> "Mike, John wants to put the book on the table, but he can't. His arm is broken. Put the book on the table for him."

Another exercise for teaching phrasal verbs that requires listening and manipulating objects is similar to the first exercise mentioned in the Listen and Respond Physically section. However, instead of having students stand up and sit down, have them manipulate objects. For example, ask a student to come to the front of the room. Put a piece of paper on the desk and say:

> "José, pick up the paper. Throw it away. Oh, oh! We want to
> keep it. Pick it up again. Give it to Marcia. She's had it long
> enough. Take it away from her."

Whether the commands are simple or complex, the same principles apply. In most classes, the teacher can even invite one of the students to take over the role of giving commands. This is usually well received by the class.

LOOK, LISTEN, AND VERBALLY RESPOND

A very effective technique taken from the Natural Approach, developed by Krashen and Terrell (1983), which we have seen Terrell skillfully demonstrate several times, involves the teacher speaking to students who can only give one-word responses (as a class or individually). The word can be *yes* or *no*, or it can be someone's name, a noun, an adjective, a number, etc. Terrell uses this technique to teach vocabulary, but it can also be used to present or practice certain structures, such as *or* questions, after students have mastered comprehension of *yes/no* and *wh*-questions.

If students already know each other's names and some basic color vocabulary, the teacher can begin by standing next to a student and asking the class (or an individual student) who it is:

> T: Is this Maria or is this Susana? (demonstrates response)
>   Susana.
> T: Is this Maria or Susana? (elicits response)
> S(s): Susana.
> T: Is Susana's blouse pink or is it blue? (points to blouse
>   and responds) Pink.
> T: Is Susana's blouse pink or blue? (elicits response)
> S(s): Pink.

This should continue with examples involving other students until the teacher is confident the class understands how to comprehend and respond to alternative questions. At this point, the teacher can introduce some well-selected pictures of desserts or sweets (along with the vocabulary if it is unfamiliar) and say, "We're going to a restaurant. We're going out for dessert." The conversation can continue as follows:

<pre>
T: Jorgé, do you want ice cream, pie, or cake?
J: Pie.
T: Do you want apple pie or cherry pie?
J: Cherry.
T: Samira, do you want ice cream, pie, or cake?
S: Ice cream.
T: Do you want vanilla ice cream or chocolate?
S: Chocolate.
</pre>

This should continue until everyone has a chance to respond. The most common error is for students to answer *yes* or *no* when they should make a specific choice. When this happens, the teacher should show pictures of all the options in the alternative question and say to the student(s), "You can't have both/all of them. You have to make a choice. Which one do you want? Do you want this one or that one?" During the exercise, the teacher should also include a few recall items, such as these:

<pre>
T: Li, I forgot. Does Jorgé want ice cream or pie?
L: Ice cream.
</pre>

If there is a mistake, as above, or any confusion, *yes/no* and *wh*-questions can be used to straighten out the facts:

<pre>
T: Is that right, Jorgé?
J: No.
T: What do you want?
J: Pie (or cherry pie).
</pre>

In this way, comprehension of alternative questions is introduced, while comprehension of *yes/no* questions and *wh*-questions is reviewed. This would take place during the presentation phase of a lesson.

LISTEN AND SPEAK

One of the best communicative exercises for practicing prepositions and phrasal verbs requires some preparation but is well worth the time and effort. Before class, you will need to cut out different shapes (triangles, circles, squares, and rectangles) from different colored papers. Make the shapes different sizes and colors, but make two copies of each color/shape combination. Use enough different shapes so that each student can have about six or eight pieces of paper. Before you

start, be sure students know the names of all the shapes and colors you
have used.

For this exercise, each student will need a partner. Each pair
is given matching sets of colored shapes. They can arrange their chairs
so they are sitting back to back. One student in each pair then arranges
his set of shapes on his desk any way he chooses. The only requirements
are that he must use all the shapes the teacher has given him, and his
partner must not be able to see the arrangement. Then, when the teacher
tells students to begin, the student with the arranged shapes must tell
his partner where to put her pieces of paper so the arrangement on
her desk exactly matches the arrangement on his. He might say things
such as:

> "Find the little yellow triangle. Put it three centimeters down
> from the left-hand side of your desk and two centimeters away
> from the top. Now find the big red circle and put it to the right
> of the triangle."

Perhaps the other student will ask:

> "Is the big circle about five centimeters in diameter?"

The first student will answer:

> "No, that's the small red circle. Find the big one."

Walk through the class as students do this exercise and make
sure they are using English. If they forget the word for a particular
shape, let them describe it as best they can, and you can present the
vocabulary they have forgotten after the exercise. Don't let the students
turn around or look at each other's arrangement until the exercise is
finished. Both students can speak and ask any questions of the other
that they want. The point is to communicate. The exercise is difficult
but offers a high return for the effort: it demands communication, encourages use of new vocabulary, practices structures already learned,
and is exceedingly challenging.

LISTEN AND WRITE

For more advanced students, there are exercises that require them to
listen and write. Several such activities are discussed in detail in Chapter
Eleven, which deals with text-based exercises, such as dictation and
dictocomp.

CONCLUSION

In this chapter we stated that listening-based exercises, such as those above, are excellent for several different reasons: First, they help the second-language learner—even the first-day beginner—match meaning and form in context; this match is achieved by techniques that get the learner to listen and respond physically or verbally, with the teacher using as resources the students, the classroom, and occasionally pictures or special objects. Second, such exercises are in tune with the principle of delayed oral production, and we think that learners who are allowed an initial silent period will be more fluent and have better pronunciation than learners required to speak immediately. Third, even if the needs of your students make a completely silent initial learning period impractical, a careful integration of listening-based exercises with the other activities in your curriculum can significantly improve the language proficiency (and this includes the grammar) of your beginning-level students (Banjar).

Since these listening exercises can be as simple or as complex as required, they can be used liberally with students at all levels of proficiency. For more advanced students, they can be part of the presentation phase, after which students can be asked to state the rule (i.e., to use inductive reasoning). For beginning students who do not have enough language to state a rule, these exercises may constitute both presentation and practice.

When doing these exercises in the classroom, don't proceed too quickly. Remember that what sounds familiar to you might be strange and difficult for your students to comprehend and distinguish. Repeat as often as necessary, but try to speak at a relatively normal pace with normal intonation, and keep in mind that there is no need to resort to ungrammatical speech or baby talk.

Although we may very well learn to speak a second language by first learning to comprehend it, remember that much more than comprehension is required if students are to develop grammatical accuracy. The remainder of this book deals with a variety of strategies that will help you take your students beyond comprehension to meaningful production, which is another necessary step for learners if their goal is achieving a reasonable level of grammatical accuracy.

·ACTIVITIES·

Discussion Questions

1. Do you think it is possible to develop listening-based exercises to present more complex structures, such as conditional sentences and relative clauses? If so, provide a brief illustration.

2. Do you feel that listening-based grammar exercises will be equally useful to second-language learners of all ages and at all levels of proficiency? Why or why not?

3. Have you ever experienced or observed a language class in which students were doing listening-based activities? If so, describe the activities.

Suggested Activities

1. Develop a listening-based grammar presentation activity for some point not covered in this chapter, such as demonstratives, the use of *not*, or the use of the present progressive tense. Share your activity with others and see what they think of it.

2. Try out the activity described in this chapter in the Listen and Speak section with a colleague, classmate, or family member. Use your native language or any language you like. Was it easy? How did it affect the quality of your communication? What did you learn from the experience?

TELLING STORIES

TEACHER-GENERATED STORIES

Everyone loves a story, including ESL students. Stories are used in contemporary ESL materials to promote communication and expression in the classroom. A dialog reflecting some version of a "story" is central to audio-lingual lessons, and Rassias (1983) has demonstrated very graphically the value of the teacher as a good storyteller in foreign-language teaching. Serial-type stories containing the structures of the lesson can be found in texts such as Praninskas (1973), among numerous others.

Stories can be used for both eliciting and illustrating grammar points. The former employs inductive reasoning, while the latter requires deductive thought, and it is useful to include both approaches in lesson planning. In addition, a well-told story is the perfect context for a structure-discourse match, but the technique can also be used effectively for a structure-social factor match. As noted in Chapter One, many techniques can be used with more than one kind of match. Storytelling is one of these extremely versatile techniques, and once you get the hang of it, it can be a convenient and natural grammar teaching tool. You may even find that it is the technique that holds students' attention best, as well as the one they enjoy most.

The ESL classroom has always attracted and provided a platform for great storytellers. However, you don't have to be Mark Twain or Will Rogers to tell a story well. Grammar points can be contexualized in stories that are absorbing and just plain fun if they are selected with the interest of the class in mind, are told with a high degree of energy,

51

and involve the students. Students can help create stories and impersonate characters in them.

Students will certainly appreciate and respond to your efforts to include them in the storytelling process, but they will also, we have found, enjoy learning about you through your stories. Adult-school students are particularly interested in their teacher; anecdotes about you, your family, or your friends, as long as they are relevant and used in moderation, can be very effective.

Stories should last from one to five minutes, and the more exaggerated and bizarre they are, the more likely students will remember the teaching points they illustrate. Let us now consider some stories that have been used in adult ESL classes to teach various grammar points.

Past Perfect

Recall that the lesson presented in Chapter Two introduced the passive voice with a story that used students in the class as the characters. This same technique, originally suggested to us and demonstrated by Randall Burger of Cambria English Institute in Los Angeles, can be used to present the past perfect. Again, the story centers around students, and student participation and development of the story is encouraged.

In an intermediate class, the story could go as follows:

"Let's say that Mrs. Gonzales gets tired of her job. What do you do, Mrs. Gonzales?"

Allow the student to respond. Then continue:

"OK. Let's say that Mrs. Gonzales is tired of working in a hospital. She wants to find a new job where she can make more money. Is that right, Mrs. Gonzales?"

Shake your head up and down to signal to Mrs. Gonzales what her response should be. The student will usually catch on immediately and respond in a way that will advance the story. If not, continue to shake your head to prompt the correct response. You might, perhaps, even give the correct response yourself, with good humor. After a few stories, you will probably find that students await your cues eagerly and respond promptly, or occasionally enjoy giving you the wrong response before agreeing to follow your cues. Both kinds of responses can be effective and serve to make the experience more interesting and fun for everyone. Continue the narration:

> "So, Mrs. Gonzales decides to get a new job. What kind of job do you think she gets?"

Let students volunteer possible jobs for Mrs. Gonzales, but reject them all. When you've exhausted all of their suggestions, continue:

> "No, these are really good ideas, but Mrs. Gonzales doesn't get any of those jobs. You're a really good cook, aren't you?"

Shake your head up and down to cue a positive response:

> "What dish do you cook best? Enchiladas? Now, Nelson, you're a rich man, aren't you?"

Shake your head up and down to cue Nelson if necessary:

> "Would you like to invest some money? Good. Why don't you give Mrs. Gonzales fifty thousand dollars to open an enchilada stand?"

Explain that with Nelson's help, Mrs. Gonzales opened an enchilada stand:

> "I think Mrs. Gonzales will make a lot of money. What do you think, Mehdi?"

After Mehdi responds:

> "Well, you know, she did just that. Mrs. Gonzales was so successful that in just six months, she had made enough money to pay Nelson back and had one hundred thousand dollars left over besides. Each year, she sold more and more enchiladas. She became a very rich woman and moved to Beverly Hills. She bought a big house with a swimming pool, and what else, Mrs. Gonzales?"

After she responds:

> "Wow! Doesn't that sound great? Well, you know, after two or three years, Mrs. Gonzales decided that she wanted to retire. She had made so much money, she didn't need any more. Now, Mrs. Gonzales, let me ask you, how much money had you made before you retired?"

With cues, get Mrs. Gonzales up to a million:

> "That's right. Mrs. Gonzales retired after she had made a million dollars."

The sentence can be written on the board and the form of the past perfect then elicited, perhaps with the aid of a time line:

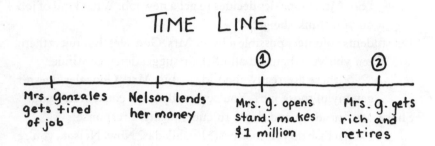

Put the number *1* over the first action, making the money, and the number *2* over the second action, retiring. Ask students what the difference in form is between the first action and the second action. You want them to notice that the first action is expressed by *had* + a past participle and that the second action is expressed in the simple past. The teacher can tell two or three more stories, write the elicited lines on the board, and point out the parallels in form. Stories based on sentences such as the following have all been successful in classes we have observed, but may have to be adapted for your students.

• Juan had repeated Level 3 four times before he passed.
• Carlos had had three girlfriends before he fell in love with Luisa.
• Marie had eaten three plates of spaghetti before she was full.
• Mr. Lee had asked a number of students before he got the correct answer.

When telling stories, as with all other aspects of teaching, the teacher must exercise good taste and caution, but still communicate with the class. The appropriate balance varies from class to class, and only individual teachers will know what the balance should be and when it must be adjusted. Once the teacher has told the stories and elicited the context and rules, the presentation, the first phase of the grammar lesson, is finished. The class should then be ready to go on to structured exercises, followed by communicative exercises (Chapter Two).

Modals

Many teachers find modal auxiliaries and perfect modals difficult to teach. They are very problematic for most students as well because, unlike other verbs in English, modals act almost like sentential operators. That is, they impart a quality of probability, obligation, etc. to the entire sentence. Therefore, to communicate the function and meaning of a modal or perfect modal, lessons must be richly contextualized with a variety of examples. Storytelling, of course, is perfectly suited to the task. To teach *must*, you might tell a story about one of your students, José:

> "Usually he's a very good student who pays close attention in class. However, today he is gazing out the window with a silly grin on his face. When I call on him, he only sighs. When I walk by his chair, I see *José + Maria*, with little hearts, written all over his notebook. What can we conclude?"

Here let the class volunteer. Then continue:

> "Obviously, José must be in love."

Write the sentence on the board, and then tell another story which will elicit the inferential use of *must*. When you have two sentences on the board with which to work, draw students' attention to the salient points.

To illustrate perfect modals, you could tell the story of one of your students after the last exam. First set up the context of the exam:

> "Last month we had an exam. Was it difficult, Mario?"

After the time period and the difficulty of the exam have been established, tell the class about René.

> "After the exam, I saw René. He was smiling and whistling. He looked very confident. He wasn't nervous at all. Now we're all very intelligent. We look at René, a good student, and we see him smiling and relaxed. What can we conclude?"

The response we are looking for here is, "He must have done very well" or "He must have passed the exam."

STUDENT-GENERATED STORIES

Our students are marvelous storytellers as well as excellent listeners, and this ability can be used to good advantage. For example, for communicative practice of the simple past, Randall Burger[1] has his

---

[1] Personal communication.

students complete the following with a story:

"Last night I got locked out of my house because . . ."

This exercise can be oral or written. Students love to use their imaginations and often can create very entertaining stories.

True stories can also be very exciting. An occasion for structured, communicative practice of the past perfect could be provided by asking students to tell their partners or the class about five things they had never done before they came to the United States. For example:

"Before I came to the United States, I had never eaten a hamburger."

Telling each other how they spend national holidays provides an opportunity for students to use the simple present. Telling about next weekend's plans will elicit the future. Conditional use of perfect modals can be practiced by discussing what students could have done if they had wanted to or whom they could have (or should have) married. Such past unreal conditionals are appropriate for discussing what would have happened if they had done so. One effective procedure is for the teacher to model a story first and then to direct students to tell their stories to their partners. Students usually find the teacher's story almost as interesting as their own, and modeling the activity seems to break the ice. It also gives students an opportunity to hear the grammatical structure in context once more before they produce it.

Modified Cloze

A short anecdote or story from which the structure under consideration is omitted can be used for focused practice of a particular grammatical structure. For example, the following story about Nasrudin provides students with an opportunity to practice the correct use of definite and indefinite articles. Omit the underlined articles, and number each blank in the story for discussion and correction purposes.

Nasrudin

Once upon a time there was a carpenter who had so much work to do that he decided he needed an assistant. He put an advertisement in the paper, and soon someone came to apply for the job. The carpenter was surprised and disappointed when a strange, weak-looking man named Nasrudin appeared at the door.

At first, the carpenter didn't want to hire Nasrudin because he didn't look like he could even lift a toothpick; however, as no one else had answered the ad, the carpenter finally said:

"OK, I'll give you a chance. Do you see the forest over there? Take my axe and chop as much lumber as you can."
At dusk Nasrudin returned, and the carpenter asked:

"How many trees have you chopped down?"

"All the trees in the forest," Nasrudin replied.
Shocked, the carpenter ran to the window and looked out. There were no trees left standing on the hillside. Nasrudin had chopped down the entire forest. The astonished carpenter asked Nasrudin:

"Where did you learn to chop lumber?"

"In the Sahara Desert," Nasrudin answered.

"That's ridiculous," laughed the carpenter. "There aren't any trees in the Sahara Desert."

"There aren't any *now*," Nasrudin replied.

Any joke or anecdote can be put to the same use if it contains examples of the structure being taught. Simply write the story in language you think your students will understand. It has been our experience that teachers usually are better judges of complexity and what their students comprehend than any formula, whether syntactic or lexical, for assessing difficulty. Sometimes it is necessary to introduce key lexical items before the activity, but these should be kept to a minimum and introduced a day or two in advance and reviewed on the day of the exercise. This allows students sufficient time to internalize the vocabulary items and gives them the opportunity to focus on form rather than on lexicon when the lesson is finally presented.

For example, one might use the old story of "The Most Intelligent Man in the World." Key lexical items in the story include *pilot*, *automatic pilot*, *stewardess*, *knapsack*, and *parachute*. These words should be introduced a day or two before the story is told. Then the teacher should write up the story, leaving numbered blanks for the structures students are to focus on and fill in. For example, if one is teaching the use of *too*, *very*, and *enough*, the structured practice story might look like this:

The Most Intelligent Man in the World

A private jet with president X, a priest, a hippie, and the most intelligent man in the world was traveling through the air when suddenly one of the engines began to cough and splutter. The pilot checked the gauge and realized that there wasn't *enough* fuel to make it to the airport. He set the plane on automatic pilot and went back to the passenger compartment. The passengers were *very* frightened when they saw the pilot. He had a parachute on, and he said:

"I'm very sorry, but we don't have *enough* fuel to make it to the airport. Unfortunately, we also don't have *enough* parachutes for everyone. I'm taking one, and the stewardess is taking another. That will leave three. The four of you will have to decide among yourselves who gets them. Don't take *too* long because you only have *enough* fuel for about three more minutes. Good-bye."

With that, the pilot and the stewardess jumped out of the plane together. President X was the first person to speak. He said to the others:

"I'm President X. I'm the president of country Y. I'm much *too* important to die. I have a lot of responsibilities, and a lot of people depend on me. I should have a parachute."

He put on one of the parachutes and jumped out of the plane. The next person to speak was the most intelligent man in the world:

"I'm the most intelligent man in the world. People come from all over the world to ask my advice. I've solved problems in every country of the world. I'm a *very* important person. I'm much *too* important to die. I'm also *very* intelligent. The world needs me more than it needs a priest or a hippie. I should have a parachute."

With that, he took a parachute and jumped out of the plane. Now there was only one parachute left. The hippie looked at the priest, but the priest didn't seem *very* upset. The priest spoke first:

"Look, I'm a man of God. I've made my peace with my maker. I'm not afraid to die. There aren't *enough* parachutes for both of us, so why don't you take this last one? Go in peace, my son."

The hippie just smiled. He was *very* relaxed and said:

"No sweat, man. There are *enough* parachutes for both of us. The most intelligent man in the world just jumped out of the plane with my knapsack."

This story has been well received by advanced students, but if it seems too dated or doesn't appeal to you, you might try another joke or even a simplified version of a classic short story by someone such as Somerset Maugham or Guy de Maupassant. Much as we might dislike comic book or simplified versions of great literature, the plots are classic and hold students' attention in a way that other stories do not. For more advanced students, a story from *Time* magazine or a local newspaper can be transformed into a valuable resource by making it a cloze exercise that focuses on the relevant grammatical structure.

A method developed by Trudy Aronson of the Cambria English Institute to teach summarizing skills is also very helpful in communicative practice of a grammar point. Short articles from sources such as *Weekly Reader*, the Laubach Literacy newspaper, or simplified news publications for ESL students are cut out and mounted on heavy paper. Students are divided into pairs, each member given a different story. Students are allowed only a few minutes to read their stories. Then they must summarize their stories for their partners. The stories can be chosen for the type(s) of structure or tense they will elicit and used accordingly. For example, non-referential *it* and the future tense can be used in summarizing a weather forecast. Feature stories often use the present tense, and some news stories are written in the simple past. Teachers should feel free to specify a particular structure or tense. Usually learners are cooperative and welcome the opportunity for communicative practice of a specific form.

CONCLUSION

Storytelling is traditional in almost all cultures. We can tap into that tradition for a very portable resource and a convenient and flexible technique for teaching any phase of a grammar lesson. A story provides a realistic context for presenting grammar points and holds and focuses students' attention in a way that no other technique can. Although some teachers are better at telling stories than others, almost any of us can tell stories with energy and interest. Students naturally like to listen to stories, and most are remembered long after the lesson is over.

· ACTIVITIES ·

Discussion Questions

1. Have you ever been in a language class, as teacher or student, in which a story was used to present a grammar point? Did it work? Why or why not?

2. What are some good sources that ESL teachers can consult for stories that lend themselves to teaching a particular structure?

3. What grammar points other than those presented in this chapter could be effectively presented in stories? (Mention at least three.)

Suggested Activities

1. Develop a story completion or modified cloze exercise that should elicit a particular structure. Ask native speakers of English (if available) to do the exercise and see if they actually use the predicted structure. If you did not get the results you expected, can you explain why?

2. Find a story, joke, or anecdote that lends itself to practice of a particular structure. Share this teaching idea with your colleagues.

3. Make up a story that illustrates a particular structure using four of your students as characters (or four of your friends if you don't currently teach). Tell this story to a colleague and watch her face for reactions as you tell the story. Did the story seem to hold her interest? After you have made your own assessment, ask your colleague what she thinks of this lesson.

4. Think of a favorite short story and retell it to your colleagues in language you think your class would understand, or write the story down and try it out on an actual ESL class. How was the story received? Can you explain why it was or was not well received? If the story was not successful, what changes should be made?

·CHAPTER FIVE·
Techniques

DRAMATIC ACTIVITIES
AND ROLEPLAY

In this chapter we will discuss a variety of dramatic techiques, including roleplay. These techniques facilitate a match between structure and social functions and can be used for both communicative and focused grammar practice. Methodologists most frequently propose arguments for using dramatic activities to teach second-language communication skills and phonology; however, we feel that these activities are an effective tool for teaching grammar as well.

Based on her experience with ESL students and her research into the use of drama in language education, psychotherapy, and speech therapy, Stern (1980) hypothesizes that dramatic activities in the classroom can be helpful in several ways. They appear to provide or increase motivation, heighten self-esteem, encourage empathy, and lower sensitivity to rejection. It is interesting to note that these same affective factors are also posited by Schumann (1975) as being critical in second-language acquisition. Therefore, it seems reasonable to assume that drama is an excellent tool for second-language teaching.

Stern maintains that dramatic activities "are a curative for the frustration and lagging interest which often occur during second-language learning," because they provide a compelling reason to learn.[1] In effect, drama gives a "strong instrumental motivation" for learning the second language. In addition, Stern reports that Heyde (1979) has correlated self-esteem or self-confidence with oral proficiency in a second language. Stern thus concludes that drama "raises self-esteem by demonstrating to second-language learners that they

---

[1] See also Hsu (1975); Via (1976); and Moulding (1978).

are indeed capable of expressing themselves in realistic communicative situations" (p. 80). In other words, dramatic activities can increase oral proficiency by increasing self-esteem.

Most second-language learners can recall at least one experience when they were reluctant to use the new language because their command of it was considerably less than native-like. According to Stern, adults are especially inhibited by embarrassment or fear of rejection. However, she points out that "several educators have found that drama creates a non-threatening situation which can reduce and even eliminate sensitivity to rejection" (p. 80).[2]

Stern also addresses the issue of empathy. Following work done by Guiora (1972), Stern thinks of empathy as a relaxation or suspension of psychological mechanisms which separate us from each other. Guiora's research suggests that empathy, or "ego flexibility," is essential to acquiring target-like pronunciation in a second language. Schumann takes this one step further by suggesting that "the natural factors which induce ego flexibility and lower inhibitions are those conditions which make the learner less anxious, make him feel accepted, and make him form positive identification with speakers of the target language" (p. 227). Stern feels that dramatic activities provide the second-language learner with just such "natural factors."

Perhaps the most exciting thing about dramatic activities is a phenomenon consistently observed by UCLA oral communication teachers and ESL students, as well as by others who have viewed videotapes from these classes. We have also observed this phenomenon during student-generated skits such as those described later in this chapter. Stern calls this the "spontaneity state." She reports that it is fairly common in psychodrama and quotes an observation made by John Mann describing it:

> In varying degrees the person in such a state acts as though inspired. He draws on resources which neither he nor his friends may have thought he had at his disposal. (Mann 1970: 7–8)

Stern speculates that perhaps this is what an ESL student observed

---

[2] See also Hines (1973); Via (1976); Early (1977); Crookall (1978).

when he said of a classmate, "The transformation in his manner was unbelievable. He really 'hammed it up' during the phone conversation and everyone in the audience noticed" (Hinofotis and Bailey 1978: 15).

The experience is really quite remarkable for students and teachers alike, and the fluency and accuracy exhibited are often amazing. Stern hypothesizes that this occurs during the spontaneity state because at that point

> . . . the usual gap between thought and expression which ceases to exist in the native language might cease to exist in the second language as well. Equally relevant to second-language learning is the "free-flowing" creativity and the ability of the person to draw upon heretofore untapped resources. (p. 85)

As Stern says, the communicative strategies students acquire during such a dramatic activity help them to "adjust to becoming a speaker of the second language and tends to become a part of their linguistic repertoire" (p. 86).

SKITS FOR ADVANCED GRAMMAR REVIEW

One of the difficulties with teaching advanced-level students is that although knowledge of certain grammatical structures is assumed, not all of the students truly command them. Moreover, it is often exceedingly difficult for the teacher to determine which structures have been internalized. A dramatic activity is an excellent tool for such an assessment. It can pinpoint which structures need to be reviewed and practiced.

Divide students into small groups of five to ten. Explain to them that they are to write a skit that they will perform for the others. If you are teaching at a small institution, the whole school can be your audience. If you are teaching at a university or adult school, probably only one or two other classes have enough in common with your students to appreciate their production. In any case, providing an audience is the task of the teacher and should be dealt with before beginning the activity. Of course, classmates constitute a sufficient audience if there are enough of them and there is adequate space to rehearse in without distracting anyone; the students themselves are enough if the production can be videotaped. An audience of some sort is essential since it stimulates motivation and provides a "payoff" for many class sessions of hard work. It is vital to tell students who the audience will consist of before they begin to work on their skit, as the audience will, to some extent, determine the content of the play. A skit prepared for classmates or schoolmates might not be appreciated by family and friends.

The first few sessions should be devoted to brainstorming, in which groups work out their ideas for skits. The teacher should act strictly as a facilitator. Allow students to create something of their own, and intervene only when it becomes apparent that no progress will be made without your assistance. If this happens and a group appears completely blocked, the teacher can suggest possibilities, such as acting out a joke or anecdote; or doing a parody on American life or institutions, such as a beauty contest, popular music, or school life; or being a foreigner in the United States. One of our groups did a mock ballet, all wearing enormous work boots; another did a spoof of the six o'clock news, complete with commercials. At this stage, students will do best if left to their own devices. The best-received skits always seem to be the ones the teacher has influenced least. Let students' imaginations go and avoid censoring. If the content of the skit is such that school administrators or some other group might be embarrassed or offended by it, speak to the potentially offended group to avoid surprises, but defend your students. We know of one class that did a good-natured spoof of one of the school's administrators that was always humorous, but sometimes unflattering. Long before the students had invested a great deal of time in their project, the teacher went to the administrator and explained what the students were planning. Fortunately, the administrator had an exceptional sense of humor and supported dramatic activities in the ESL classroom, as well as the students' creative self-expression. Performed before the entire school, the play was an unqualified hit. Years later, students still remember their lines, and actors and audience alike have characterized the performance as one of the richest and most positive experiences of their time in the United States. If your circumstances do not permit this much freedom, another activity might be more appropriate since freedom of expression is essential to the success of a student-generated skit.

After one or two planning sessions, it is time for the groups to work on an actual script. Make sure they write down the dialog for their skit and plan the necessary costumes, makeup, and props. It is best to limit these to things that can be brought in from home. Elaborate sets are not necessary, but creative costumes, makeup, and simple props make all the difference in the world. Give students about three sessions to work on this step. During the first two steps, English is being used for communicative purposes, and the teacher should not correct errors or interrupt any creative work. She should make unobtrusive notes on grammatical errors or lexical difficulties and organize minigrammar lessons (see page 145) around those points.

The next step is for the teacher to edit students' work so that the language is idiomatic and grammatically correct. This is an assessment step and is essential, as it provides a clear picture of which structures need review. Recurrent structural errors and poor word choice can provide the basis for grammar lessons during the remainder of the semester, and you will also have a ready-made context (the dramatic activity) for each lesson. Thus, such activities become contexts for grammar lessons that your students will usually remember.

One aspect of editing involves meeting with groups in order to determine what they are trying to say. They might also need a little help with ending a scene, planning a prop, or dressing a character. During all of this interaction, both written and spoken, the teacher should be alert to grammatical errors and take careful notes for future lessons.

Once the script has been completed, type it up and make enough copies for all of the actors and yourself. Students now need to rehearse. One hour of rehearsal daily for three or four weeks is not too much. Concurrently, grammar lessons should be conducted on what the teacher has determined needs review.

When students are rehearsing, the teacher can act as a director by suggesting movements, delivery of lines, etc. He can move around from group to group and spend about ten or fifteen minutes with each one. After a week of rehearsal, the teacher should begin to correct pronunciation. Students should be encouraged to put their lines on tape, and deliver them in front of mirrors, roommates, parents, pets, or anyone who will listen. They should be allowed to correct each other and be reminded to speak clearly so that they can be understood by their audience.

Have each group rehearse its production numerous times. Every rehearsal reinforces grammar points and helps offset stage fright. As the performance approaches, students suddenly realize they are nervous. Stage fright can be assuaged to a great degree by preparation. If creative control is left to the students, they will not become bored or lose interest.

The next step is a full dress rehearsal in front of a small audience. Perhaps you can recruit a colleague or two who have a free period, a counselor, or a secretary. Guests at dress rehearsals are usually very effusive. Praise and encouragement put students in a positive frame of mind for the final performance.

On the day of the performance, give your students plenty of time to get into costume and prepare. Make sure you have a flash camera and at least one roll of film, and invite the school's officials. Introduce each skit (but let your students take their bows alone) and prepare to experience one of the most rewarding moments in your teaching career. It may seem elaborate, but a dramatic activity is a remarkably effective way to diagnose and remedy problems with grammar that advanced students are supposed to have mastered, but haven't.

TRANSCRIBED CONVERSATIONS

Another ambitious but considerably less involved activity is the use of transcribed conversations that illustrate the grammar point(s) you are teaching, but in the context of natural speech. This is not an activity for diagnosis and remedy such as the one above, but one which leads to communicative practice of a grammar point.

There are a number of sources for transcribed speech, such as *Informal Speech* (Carterette and Jones 1974) or *The White House Transcripts* (1974). You can also enlist the assistance of friends and family and record and transcribe conversations from parties, luncheons, and casual get-togethers. Once you explain that you are interested in natural, everyday speech and that the speakers should *not* try to avoid grammatical lapses or slang, most people will be enthusiastic about giving you a hand. At first, despite your advice to the contrary, they will probably monitor their speech. After a few minutes, however, most people forget all about the tape recorder, speak naturally, and provide you with the kind of sample you need. What you are interested in obtaining is natural, unmonitored native speech, with whatever errors, false starts, and idiosyncracies that naturally occur. Many ESL professionals believe that such authentic materials are more helpful than the usual contrived ESL texts or dialogs. After you have collected an hour or two of conversation, small exchanges that illustrate the particular grammar structure being taught can be extracted, typed up and duplicated, written on the board or an overhead projector, or given as a dictation. Students then have an authentic dialog to work with.

When working with authentic speech, it is important to make your students aware of register and discrepancies between prescriptive grammar and actual spoken English. The register in a segment from *The White House Transcripts* might be appropriate for addressing the president, but inappropriate for students addressing each other. Likewise, native speakers are likely to say, "There's some papers on the table," but write, *There are some papers on the table.* Authentic language materials are excellent for illustrating this hard-to-grasp point.

The following dialog taken from *The White House Transcripts* can be used to practice hypothetical conditional sentences. The hint of intrigue makes it all the more interesting, though few of us have the opportunity to discuss national security leaks, real or imagined.

> P: What would you say if they said, "Did you ever do any wiretapping?" That is a question they will ask. Were you aware of any wiretapping?
>
> E: Yes.
>
> P: You would say, "Yes." Then, "Why did you do it?" You would say it was ordered on a national security basis.
>
> E: National security. We had a series of very serious national security leaks. (p. 236)

When using a dialog from authentic speech, make sure you give students some idea of the context of the dialog. In our example above, one could explain that two public figures are discussing how to justify their illegal wiretapping, which they fear will shortly be uncovered.

The demise of the audio-lingual method is responsible, at least in part, for the decline in the use of the memorized dialog. However, even though memorizing stilted and contrived lines bores students and is unlikely to lead to the spontaneous generation of language, there is no evidence that repetition with sustained interest and the opportunity for elaboration is harmful; in fact, it has been our experience that this is a very natural part of language learning. Authentic dialogs can be particularly useful in the focused practice phase of a grammar lesson, especially if they are accompanied by the original tapes. (If the originals are unavailable, have native-speaking friends help you make a realistic recording.) Let students work in pairs, and have them try their best to approximate native-speaker pronunciation and intonation. Then let them record their own version of the dialog and compare it to the original. The teacher should walk around the room and listen carefully to each pair's observations. Discuss the differences students have noticed and give individual help as needed. After about twenty minutes, have students change partners, rehearse, and record again. Repeat the procedure. As a final step, have volunteer pairs perform the dialog in front of the class. Then play the original and let the class discuss differences between their classmates' performances and the conversation of the native speakers. This allows students to observe as well as produce the grammatical structures being practiced. Notice that this grammar lesson incorporates writing (if you dictate the dialog), reading, listening, and pronuciation, as well as numerous opportunities for repetition.

The final step is improvisation. This is the communicative practice phase of your lesson. For example, the teacher can tell students to set up a parallel but novel situation. Instead of saying, "What would you do if asked, 'Did you ever do any wiretapping?' " they could fill in their own variations (e.g., "What would you do if . . .?"). These might be humorous, such as "What would you do if Brooke Shields walked in right now?" or serious, such as "What would you do if your girl/boyfriend asked you to marry her/him?" The possibilities are limitless. Let students construct their own responses as well and present their improvisations in front of the class.

ROLEPLAYING

Another dramatic activity with which we are all familiar is roleplaying. According to Rosensweig (1974), "Roleplaying is the dramatization of a real-life situation in which the students assume roles. It . . . presents the students with a problem, but instead of reaching a group concensus in solving it, the students act out their solution" (p. 41). Rosensweig argues that correctly chosen roleplaying scenes expose students to the types of situations they are most likely to encounter inside and outside of the classroom. Feedback from the teacher provides them with the linguistic and cultural awareness needed to function in such situations, thus improving their self-confidence and ability to communicate effectively. It is an excellent technique for communicative practice of structures sensitive to social factors.

The general procedure he suggests is first to hand out the problem to the students and answer questions. Next, introduce and explain the vocabulary and structures necessary for the task. In the following session, divide students into groups, in which they discuss and practice how they are going to do the roleplay. Rosensweig suggests that during this step the teacher allow students to communicate freely and not interrupt for correction. However, the teacher should take notes on grammatical, cultural, and phonological errors for subsequent treatment. Next, the roleplay is performed before the class. After each enactment, the teacher comments on selected minor language errors. Major errors are saved for formal grammar lessons later. After each group has performed, the entire class discusses the questions raised by the situation, such as different interpretations of the scene and culturally or linguistically appropriate responses. The last step is to assign a writing exercise based on the roleplay or a related question. Subsequent grammar lessons based on the errors observed during the exercise should be presented.

Rosensweig suggests that the entire exercise be spread out over three days: introducing the roleplay situation and the initial group work on the first day; more group work, performances, class evaluations, and written work on the second day; and the grammar follow-up on the third. He points out that a classroom activity such as this usually includes work on vocabulary, a culture lesson, written work, and a grammar lesson, as well as work on pronunciation and communicative strategies.

To illustrate the procedure, let us consider the following roleplay from Rosensweig. The grammar focus is the social use of modals, such as *May I see your driver's license, please?*, *Would you mind stepping over here, please?*, and the logical use of modals, as in *I must have left my insurance verification at home* or *The light might have been yellow*.

Being Stopped by a Police Officer
(*Student Handout*)

I. *Scene*

You are driving down a freeway in California and you are stopped by a police officer. He is completely unsympathetic to the fact that you are a foreign student and your nervousness makes it difficult for you to express yourself. You are not sure why he has stopped you, but you know that he is extremely angry. Your are to work out a short skit with three characters: the driver, a passenger, and the police officer (a fourth character could be another police officer). The presentation should be approximately five minutes.

II. *Vocabulary*

driver's license	ticket
vehicle registration	citation
insurance	to break the law
license plate	to step out of the car
valid until _____	rearview mirror
(date)	

III. *Questions for planning your roleplaying*
- Why has the police officer stopped you?
- How should you react to his anger?
- Is it possible that he had a good reason to stop you?
- What is the best way to deal with the matter?
- What kind of language do you use when you talk to a police officer?
- What are the possible problems you might have (expired license, forgetting an important document, something wrong with the car)?

IV. *Discussion Questions*
- Is bribery a good way to deal with a police officer in the United States? Why or why not?
- What is the role of a police officer in the United States? In your country?

- What is the best way to treat a police officer in the United States?
- If you are stopped by a police officer, how should you act?
- Would you act the same way if you were stopped by a police officer in your country? What would you do differently?

V. *Suggested Topics for Writing*

  1. Recount a personal experience that you have had with a police officer in the United States. (This is particularly suited for practicing the past tense and the narrative mode.)
  2. Compare and contrast the role of a police officer in the United States with the role of a police officer in your country. (This would elicit the present tense, expository mode.)

CONCLUSION

In this chapter we have discussed dramatization, a technique that is particularly appropriate for teaching grammatical structures that are sensitive to social factors. We have also proposed this technique for pinpointing grammatical structures which should have been mastered by high-intermediate and advanced students, but were not. Our resources have included roleplays, dialogs, transcribed conversations, and skits. In addition to facilitating a match between structure and social factors and diagnosing gaps in grammatical knowledge, these activities provide meaningful contexts for integrating writing, reading, pronunciation, listening, and grammar. They also enable students to operate spontaneously with the language, as well as experience increased empathy, heightened self-esteem and motivation, and lowered sensitivity to rejection, thus facilitating second-language acquisition. Finally, dramatic activities, if properly conducted, provide teachers with delightful lessons and provide students with some of the richest and most memorable experiences they have in their struggle with the second language.

·ACTIVITIES·

Discussion Questions

1. Have you ever participated in a class, as a teacher or student, in which dramatic activities were used? What was done? Was it effective? Why or why not?

2. What were the four personality traits that Schumann suggested might make second-language learning easier? Do you agree? Explain how you think the presence or absence of these personality traits might affect learning grammar.

3. What kinds of teachers or learners might be uncomfortable with dramatic activities in the ESL/EFL classroom? In this type of situation, should dramatic activities be omitted altogether? Why or why not?

Suggested Activities

1. Select one of the dramatic activities suggested in this chapter, or devise one of your own. Try it out on your colleagues and then evaluate the results.

2. Select several short scenes from various plays and look through them to see what kinds of grammatical structures could be taught by exploiting three different scenes.

3. Persuade some of your friends to allow you to tape their free conversation. Then play it back and see what kind of grammar lesson you could organize around a segment of the conversation.

PICTURES

Pictures are versatile and useful resources for teaching aspects of grammar that require a structure-meaning match, and in this chapter we will suggest several areas of grammar for which pictures constitute particularly effective resources. They can be used in all phases of a grammar lesson (i.e., in presentation, focused practice, communicative practice, and for feedback and correction). Interesting or entertaining pictures motivate students to respond in ways that more routine teaching aids, such as a textbook or a sentence on the board, cannot. Although they can be used to advantage at all levels of proficiency, they are especially useful with beginning and low-intermediate learners, who sometimes have trouble understanding long or complicated verbal cues.

Pictures can also be used in various configurations to enhance learning and practice. They introduce a great deal of variety into the classroom. A picture may focus on one specific object, such as a house, or on an event, such as a boy jumping a fence; alternatively, a picture may evoke an entire story (e.g., a Norman Rockwell print). Between these two extremes, there are pictures of a few people or a few objects.

Pictures can be presented in pairs: the same object or person on two different occasions (e.g., Mr. Jones before and after his diet) or two different objects or people (e.g., a comb and a brush, a brother and a sister, etc.). Pictures can be grouped into semantically related sets that contain from ten to twenty items, representing animals, vehicles, flowers, fruits, etc. Finally, a picture can become part of a sequence of pictures that tells a story, much as comic strips or photo novels do. Using pictures of this type allows the teacher to focus on temporal forms and sequences in the target language.

73

In addition to eliciting verbal responses, pictures can form the basis for pair and group activities. When students move into pairs or groups, or come to the front of the class for an activity, there is appropriate physical movement (as opposed to such inappropriate activities as private conversation, passing of notes, shooting of rubber bands, staring at walls, or looking out windows). Even the most mature, highly motivated, and disciplined students have to move about a little during class. Activities that encourage appropriate movement—involving students directly or as observers—will promote and enhance active learning. We feel that pictures can play an important role in this process.

GROUP WORK AS A TECHNIQUE

Before continuing, perhaps we should say a word about group work as a technique, since in many of the activities we suggest for focused practice and communicative practice we have students working in groups or pairs. Pair or group activities demand that the teacher prepare all materials in advance and plan pair or group assignments well, so students can perform their tasks efficiently. If group work is not well planned, students become confused and demand a great deal of attention simply because they are trying to understand the task. The classroom becomes quite chaotic when ten or more groups are demanding clarification or additional directions for a task. Under such circumstances, it becomes virtually impossible for the class to work or for the teacher to move around the room and check each group's progress.

When students first begin doing group and pair work, the teacher should not expect them to form optimal groupings without assistance. Thus, in addition to carefully planning and explaining the task, the teacher must also think about group dynamics (e.g., how best to form the groups for learning). Initially, the teacher might plan the groupings in advance and project them on a transparency that, like a map, indicates the membership and location of each group. If the class is mixed ethnically, the teacher may decide to separate people with the same native language. Some teachers have found it useful to put inhibited students together so they are forced to speak.

While students are working in pairs or groups, the teacher should circulate to verify that the activity is being done as planned and to assist students who are having problems. (Students should be instructed in advance to raise their hands if they have a question or wish assistance.) The teacher should not remain seated or uninvolved during such activities but oversee as many of the pairs or groups as possible and respond or intervene as needed. From our experiences, students are less resistant to group work when the teacher is an active observer and facilitator.

As the teacher circulates, she should take notes on the errors students are making —especially the systematic errors. Such information can be used in brief follow-up exercises in which students are shown their most frequent and salient errors and invited to correct them and practice the problematic forms.

We will now present several exercises and activities in which pictures play a central role in the teaching of grammar.

USING PICTURES TO TEACH SPECIFIC STRUCTURES

Yes/No Questions

Pictures can be effective for presentation and structured practice of *yes/no* questions. One of our favorite contexts is a pet shop. For this you will need large pictures that everyone can see of 10 or 12 animals that are possible pets (e.g., a dog, a cat, a pony, a goldfish, a turtle, a canary, a parrot, a hamster, a monkey, a snake). After everyone is familiar with the vocabulary for all the animals, the teacher has one student come to the front of the room and secretly "buy" one of the pets. (If your class is small enough, have the student sit in the center of a circle formed by his classmates.) Then the classmates must guess which pet the student has purchased by asking *yes/no* questions until someone guesses the correct pet. (Note that this format is simple, in that students directly guess the names of the pets; different question forms are possible):

Classmate 1: Did you buy the monkey? Is it the monkey?
Student: No.
Classmate 2: Did you buy the dog? Do you have the dog?

Student: No.
Classmate 3: Is it the pony? Do you have the pony?
Student: Yes.

The classmate who guesses the right pet then goes to the front and makes the next secret purchase. This can continue for as long as such practice is useful. The activity can be made more demanding by allowing students to ask background questions about the pets (e.g., "Is it a large animal?" "Can it fly?") or by requiring the class to guess the price of the pet. For adult classes, instead of animals the teacher could propose trips or meals as the context. ("Did you go to Brazil?" "Did you have pizza?")

A similar though more complex and more communicative question-asking activity can be done with pictures of famous characters or personalities—real or fictional, living or dead. The important thing is that everyone in the class must immediately recognize each famous personality. In larger or low-level classes, one student comes up and selects from the pictures the "person" he will pretend to be (e.g., Napoleon). The class then asks *yes/no* questions until someone correctly guesses the identity of the student:

Classmate 1: Are you alive?
Student: No.
Classmate 2: Are you a man?
Student: Yes.
Classmate 3: Did you really exist?
Student: Yes.
Classmate 4: Were you an American?
Student: No.

In smaller and more advanced classes, the teacher can pin small pictures of personalities on each student's back. The students then have to ask their classmates *yes/no* questions in an attempt to figure out who they are (i.e., who the pictures represent). This can be done with one student asking questions of the whole class or a small group, or it can be done as a freer activity in which everyone circulates around the room and talks to everyone else.

Yes/No and Wh-questions

In an activity that provides communicative practice of both *yes/no* and *wh*-questions with reference to location, pairs of students are given two mismatched pictures of a bedroom. Students must be told in advance not to look at each other's pictures. The two pictures contain, among other things, some identical objects in different positions. The task of the students is to discover through oral communication and then to write down (a) which objects are in both bedrooms and which are not; and (b) which appear in the same location and which do not. The questions students would have to ask each other many times in the course of this activity include:

    S1: Is there a _____ in your bedroom?
    S2: No, do you have a _____ in yours?
    S1: Yes, I have a _____.
    S2: Where is the _____ (in your bedroom)?

After the oral and written work is completed, students should compare their lists against the actual pictures to see whether they have communicated effectively.

Tense and Time

To elicit structured practice of the simple present tense (habitual action), the teacher gives each group of four students a grid with eight rectangles. A specific time of day is indicated at the top of each rectangle:

Bob's Schedule

6:45 a.m.	7 a.m.	7:45 a.m.	9 a.m.
12:15 p.m.	12:30 p.m.	2:30 p.m.	4:30 p.m.

The groups are also given 10 picture cards showing Bob engaged in various activities. For example:

- get up
- get dressed
- go to school
- talk to his girlfriend
- attend class
- fix breakfast
- eat lunch
- work out at the gym
- study in the library
- read the newspaper

To ensure that there is some variety in group accounts and some negotiation among students, each group is told to use only eight of the ten pictures to match Bob's activities with times of the day on the grid. The task is to negotiate what Bob does every day at each time specified on the grid, and this elicits the simple present tense.

Student 1: What does Bob do at 6:45?

Student 2: He fixes breakfast.

Student 3: No, first he gets up. Then he fixes breakfast.

Student 4: OK. He gets up at 6:45 and fixes breakfast at 7:00,
What does he do at 7:45?

Because the groups choose slightly different sets of eight pictures and order the pictures somewhat differently, there are variations in Bob's schedule among the groups. It can be amusing (and also a good review) to have one person from each group relate their version of Bob's daily activities. By changing the task, other tenses can be practiced using the same materials:

- Describe what Bob did yesterday. (simple past)
- Describe what Bob is going to do tomorrow. (*going to* future)

Another activity uses old photographs as a context for communicative practice of past states or habits, contrasted with current ones. The teacher should ask each of the students, well in advance of this activity, to bring in a photograph of family members or friends. The photo should be at least five years old. Not all students will have or want to share such photos, but if several students oblige these photos can form the basis for contrasting past habits and states with present ones. First, students share the photos with the class. (An opaque projector would help; otherwise, pass them around quickly. The teacher should bring plastic pockets or plastic wrap to protect the photos from finger prints and smudges.)

Next, students provide data about the photos: the names of everyone pictured, what each was doing then, and what each is doing now. These data provide the stimulus for structured practice of the habitual past tense in contrast with the simple present or the present progressive. For example:

"Seven years ago, Ricardo used to be short, but he isn't anymore. He's tall now."

"Seven years ago, Ricardo's sister Catarina used to be a student, but now she's a dentist."

"Seven years ago, Ricardo's cousin Juan used to go to high school. Now he works in a bank."

Ricardo   Catarina   Juan

This can begin as a teacher-directed activity with the whole class participating and then can change to a group-work activity, in which a student in each group describes his picture.

To elicit a discussion of travel plans using the *will* future and *because* of reason, the teacher asks students to bring in a picture postcard of some scenic place in their homeland or any place in the world of interest to them. (The teacher should have some extra postcards available.) Each student presents a card and gives a short narrative about travel plans or suggestions using the *will* future and *because* to signal a reason. The teacher should give the class a few examples so they know what to do. For example, students with cards from their homeland can say something like this:

"When *(1) the name of another student* comes to visit me in my country, I will take *(2) him/her* to see _____ *(3)* _____ because _____ *(4)* _____ . We will also visit _____ *(5)* _____ and _____ *(6)* _____ because _____ *(7)* _____ ."

Students with a card from another country can say:

"When I travel to _____ *(1)* _____ , I will visit _____ *(2)* _____ because _____ *(3)* _____ . I will also visit _____ *(4)* _____ and _____ *(5)* _____ because _____ *(6)* _____ ."

If students are at a low level, story frames such as those above can be written on the board or projected for focused practice. With more advanced students, it should suffice for the teacher to model the patterns once or twice, in which case the practice becomes more communicative.

Sequential Logical Connectors

In addition to their usefulness in teaching tense and time, a series of pictures that tells a story can be used for communicative practice of conjunctions and subordinators that overtly mark the sequence of events in a narrative.

In our first example activity, which focuses on the use of *before* and *after*, each pair of students is given two pictures representing the same person or object at two different points in time; for example, Sam weighing 300 lbs. and Sam weighing 130 lbs. or Sally's shiny car and Sally's car after an accident. The pair of students have to negotiate an understanding of which of the two events depicted occurred first and what happened between the first and second events. (Actually, in all cases either order is possible.) The pair then shows its two pictures to the class and tells the story. Students should be instructed to

use either *before* or *after* at least once in their stories. For example,
one student might say:

> "Sam decided he was too fat. He went on a diet. After he lost
> a lot of weight, he looked much better."

Another pair might describe the story this way:

> "Sam was a handsome young man. Then his girlfriend cancelled
> their engagement and left town. After that, he was so depressed
> he ate and ate and became very fat."

In an activity that allows practice of expressions of temporal sequence,
such as *first*, *then*, and *next*, each group is given an identical set of four
to six pictures in random order that tell a story. The groups must first
reorder the pictures so they tell the story and then write up a group
account using temporal transitional expressions to reinforce the
sequence of events. Some of the cards used to practice tenses in the
earlier exercise describing Bob's daily activities can be used here. For
example:

> "Bob got up early this morning. First he got dressed; then he
> fixed breakfast; then he . . ."

One member from each group then shows the pictures and reads the
story developed by his group. Alternatively, the groups can write their
stories on transparencies and each story can be put on an overhead
projector. The groups will then see if they have all reconstructed the
same sequence. Often, at least one of the groups has decided on a different order, which in turn can stimulate further discussion of whether
one sequence seems more logical (or perhaps more humorous) than
another. For example, in the example above, it's possible to say that
Bob had breakfast before he got up. It would be less logical (but perhaps
more humorous) to have Bob follow this sequence.

Comparison

Pictures of two different people (stick figures or magazine cutouts will
do) can create a context for structured or communicative practice of
comparisons. The teacher should give each pair of students two such
pictures, along with data for each picture specifying the person's name,
age, height, weight and other pertinent information. Without access
to each other's pictures or written data, both students should share
their information orally and generate a series of sentences comparing
the two people in their pictures. For example:

> "Bill is taller than George." "George is older than Bill."

For the presentation phase, the teacher should show the pictures and model the sentences. For structured practice, the frames would be provided and students would produce the sentences:

"Bill is _____ George."

"George is _____ Bill."

For communicative practice, students sit back to back so they cannot see each other's pictures. The two students thus have to ask each other many questions and share a lot of information:

S1: I have a picture of George. And you?

S2: I have a picture of Bill.

S1: George is thirty years old.

S2: Bill is twenty-five, so George is older.

A communicative activity using pictures that will help students practice the superlative degree requires groups of three. Each group receives a set of three pictures of objects such as houses or other buildings—one picture for each student—and students are told not to look at each other's pictures. Each group is also given an exercise sheet with a list of cues for questions that must be asked and answered during the activity. For example:

---

1. Most rooms?
    Q:
    A:
2. Fewest rooms?
    Q:
    A:
3. Oldest?
    Q:
    A:
4. Newest?
    Q:
    A:
5. Biggest garage?
    Q:
    A:
6. Smallest garage?
    Q:
    A:

The first group to correctly complete their exercise sheet wins. A token prize for each of the three winners, such as a piece of candy, is a nice touch.

Relative Clauses

For communicative practice of the identification function of restrictive relative clauses, the teacher gives each pair of students two identical pictures depicting four or five men, women, cars, or buildings. On one picture proper names or noun descriptions appear below each person or object; the other picture has blanks. Having been instructed not to look at his partner's picture, the student whose picture has blanks must elicit the names by asking questions with relative clauses or reduced relative clauses. For example:

"What's the name of the lady wearing the dark blue coat?"

"What the name of the lady who's laughing?"

To practice the same type of relative clause in an imperative rather than a *wh*-question, the teacher gives each group of four students four or five pictures representing semantically related nouns (e.g., different boys, houses, cars). One student in each group holds the picture cards, while another gives commands with relative clauses indicating the disposition of the pictures. For example:

"Give the picture of the boy who is playing baseball to Max."

"Put the picture of the boy who is swimming on my desk."

It might be a good idea for the teacher to do this group activity once with the whole class before the group work starts. Also, once each group has finished practicing with its own set of pictures, the groups in the classsroom can exchange picture sets. Then the other two students in each group will have a chance to hold the pictures and give the commands.

Reviewing Several Different Structures

Pictures can also be used to effectively review a week's worth of lessons. Randall Burger draws a big policewoman apprehending a small criminal on an artist's pad in front of the class as his students watch. This immediately captures their attention and interest. After he finishes, he asks questions which will elicit responses with a specific grammatical form. For example, he might ask the following questions (form elicited is in parentheses):

- What is she? (copula)
- What is she wearing? (present progressive)
- What does he do? (present tense)
- (pointing to gun) What does she have here? (present tense with stative verbs)
- Have you ever seen one? (present perfect)
- Do you have one? (present with stative verbs)
- How long has she been a policewoman? (present perfect)
- Does she make a lot of money? (negative)
- Would you like to marry her? (modal-like forms)
- What was he doing when she caught him? (past progressive)
- Do you have policewomen in your country? (*yes* or *no*)
- What would you do if you met one? (present unreal conditional)

The list of questions is, of course, limitless. The questions can be varied to focus on whatever grammatical forms the teacher would like to review. It is important that the picture be interesting and/or amusing, though a picture appropriate for one group may not be appropriate for another. Also, be sure to end the exercise before students become bored or tired of looking at the picture.

CONCLUSION

In this chapter we have shown that pictures are a very effective resource for getting students to match form with meaning. A case was made for using pictures to present or practice a wide variety of structures.

Because pictures make the learning of grammar, not to mention vocabulary, pronunciation, and other teaching points stimulating, even pleasurable, all ESL teachers should have their own picture file, especially if a good collection of such materials is not readily available for classroom use.

In addition, teachers should also draw pictures on the board and on overhead transparencies (or have students do such drawings) to encourage more practice and participation. But the teacher should always understand that when pictures are used to stimulate communicative use of a particular form, the teacher must attend to the forms students produce and, as needed, employ feedback and correction techniques such as those suggested on pages 28 and 36.

·ACTIVITIES·

Discussion Questions

1. Why do the authors feel that pictures are useful for teaching grammar? Do you agree? Give reasons for your answer.

2. What would be some good ways to file and store pictures for teaching ESL?

3. What sources of pictures other than magazines could ESL teachers consult to find pictures for use in their classes?

Suggested Activities

1. Find an interesting picture in a magazine or some other source. Identify the structure(s) you could teach using the picture.

2. If you could identify students in your current or prospective classes who could draw well or who were good photographers, list and describe two ways in which you would use the skills and interests of these students to teach grammar using their pictures or photographs.

3. Think of at least two structures other than the ones presented in this chapter that you could teach by using pictures. Describe the kinds of pictures and the activities you would use.

·CHAPTER SEVEN·

Resources

REALIA AND THE CLASSROOM

As a result of her research into memory and second-language learning, Barbara Schumann (1981) makes the following suggestions (among others) to ESL teachers:

1. In curriculum planning, allow for organization of subject matter which leads students from the familiar to a closely related but unfamiliar concept.
2. Aid students in organizing input via imagery and rehearsal situations in which the student must elaborate on what is presented.
3. Organize input in such a way that it is meaningful for the student and can be integrated with already existing knowledge and experience; experience is central to learning.
4. Provide practice situations which involve use of conscious processes and allow students to think about and generate associations and relationships between original input and novel situations by providing spaced practice. (pp. 62–63)

All of these objectives can be met quite straightforwardly by what Heaton (1979) characterizes as "an associative bridge between the classroom and the world," namely realia, an old and versatile resource of language teachers (p. 45). Before we proceed any further, a discussion of terms is in order.

Kelly (1976) states that there is some disagreement in the literature as to exactly what constitutes realia. It can refer either to objects in the learner's own environment used to illustrate vocabulary in the L-2 or to objects specific to the culture of the L-2 used for the same purpose. In the spirit of the former definition, we shall use the term to refer to objects of any origin used to illustrate vocabulary and structure in the L-2.

According to Kelly, the use of realia in language teaching has a long history. As he points out:

> The first clear information of the use of objects of general relevance comes from Tudor England. Sir Thomas Elyot, for instance, remarks, "there can be nothyng more convenient than by little and little to trayne and exercise them in speaking of Latin; infourmyng them to know first the names in Latin of all thynges that cometh in syght, and to name all the parts of their bodies" (364: 33). In the famous scene from *Henry V* in which Princess Katharine's maid tries to teach her some English, we see a little of the practical application of Elyot's advice in the Tudor classroom. (p. 13)

Realia has many uses in the classroom, not the least of which are promoting cultural insight and teaching a life-skills lexicon. Realia can also be used effectively in teaching grammar, especially for a form-meaning match. For this kind of match, realia can be used in combination with techniques such as storytelling and roleplay in both the presentation phase and the practice phase of the lesson.

USING REALIA

Hollywood Stars

Let's begin by looking at some ways realia can be used in the presentation phase. For example, if one is teaching a lesson on the copula with predicate nominals, usually a lesson for beginning students, realia can help focus students' attention as well as illustrate the point.

For this lesson, the teacher should bring in several items from a thrift store, garage sale, or child's toy box, such as a blond Halloween wig, a train engineer's hat, a stethoscope from a toy doctor's kit, and perhaps a doll. Call five students to the front of the class, put the wig on one, and say, "She's a movie star." Put the hat on another student and say, "He's an engineer." Put the stethoscope around another's neck and say, "She's a doctor." Give the doll to the last student and explain, "He's the father." Very quickly students in front will get into the spirit of the lesson and enjoy demonstrating their acting skills.

One teacher who uses this technique with his beginning students says that at this point in the lesson, the class is usually very attentive but high-spirited. He advises student teachers not to be disturbed by students' laughter, but enjoy their antics and laugh along with them. This sets up a context, an experience for the grammar point: the more students enjoy the lesson, the easier it will be for them to recall it later. During his presentation, the teacher waits until the class settles down a bit and then goes back to the student with the blond wig and asks the class, "What is she?" After a student answers that she is a movie star, he repeats the same routine with the other "actors" in front of the room, keeping the activity light and fast-paced. Although students may be more interested in the roles their classmates are playing, they are also practicing the copula.

Once students seem confident, the props can be changed to illustrate the plural (*doctors, fathers*, etc.) and the teacher can illustrate *You are students* by indicating the class as a whole. Such realia, combined with the physical movement of trading props and directing the class's attention to different actors, holds students' interest. Humor also makes the input meaningful and enables students to integrate it with knowledge and experience already acquired. The sight of a classmate in a wig is easy to visualize and provides an image that students can associate with the grammatical concept. When dolls or stethoscopes are given to two people instead of one, and the form becomes *fathers* or *doctors*, students have the opportunity to think about and generate associations and relationships between the original input and a novel situation.

You can also vary the copula lesson with the use of Halloween masks (e.g., *This is Frankenstein, She is Snow White*, etc.). Alternatively, you can use masks to practice predicate adjectives that convey emotion in sentences, such as *He is sad* or *They are happy*. Any realia that students associate with a predicate adjective (e.g., *old, young, fat, thin, intelligent, beautiful, strong*) or with any persona (e.g., *a doctor, a lawyer, a teacher*) can be used to practice the copula. Teachers can even draw masks in class rather than buy the usual commercial Halloween variety.

These same props can be used for negation. Recall that there are two distinct possibilities in English for sentential negation—either post-copula or post-auxiliary negation, as illustrated below:

1. post-copula: Judy *isn't* here.

2. post-auxiliary: Mary *doesn't* have a car.
However, English has lexical negation as well:

3. lexical: Martha is an *unhappy* person.

It makes sense to teach only one pattern at a time. For example, using the props from the exercise above, the teacher can ask (while pointing at the doctor), "Is she a movie star?" The class should respond, "No, she isn't." The teacher can then ask (while pointing at the doctor), "Is she a doctor?" thereby triggering the more frequently occurring affirmative short response, "Yes, she is."

To present sentential negation with *do* support, a situation will have to be created in which the negation of some main verb other than the copula is elicited. Students can again be called to the front of the room and each one given a familiar item. For example, one can be given a book, another a pencil, another a pen, another a notebook, another a purse, etc. The teacher can then point to the student who has the notebook and ask, "Does he have the purse?" In American English, the answer requires sentential negation (*No, he doesn't*).

Sentential negation can also be elicited by bringing two students to the front of the room and listing items of clothing they are wearing behind them on the board: red shirt, brown sweater, black shoes, etc. One can then ask about the student with the brown sweater, "Does he have a red shirt?" Another list can be made of things that obviously neither student has. It could include some humorous items, such as pink socks or a Rolls Royce. Questions about this list will elicit sentential negation in the plural (*They don't have pink socks*).

Puppets

Puppets can be used to teach the copula with predicate adjectives. Call a student to the front of the class and put a puppet on his hand. Say to the puppet, "You are sad." Act out *sad* until the student gets the idea and makes his puppet act accordingly. Call another student and get her to do the same thing. Now you can demonstrate and say, "They are sad," as well as "He is sad." You can ask the student what's wrong, eliciting the response, "I am sad."

Puppets can also be used to illustrate the meaning of adverbs of manner. For example, the teacher can say, "Judy dances gracefully" and "Punch dances clumsily"; the students manipulating the puppets will then take them through the proper movements to show that they understand the adverbs. Hand puppets also have the advantage of encouraging capable but inhibited students. Frequently, shy students will practice language more willingly when hiding behind a puppet than they will without a guise.

Identical Boxes

The presentation phase of teaching demonstratives can also make effective use of realia. The teacher needs two identical and interesting objects, such as two brightly colored boxes. She then places one box close to her and one far away. Again, the teacher's movement, as well as curiosity about the boxes, will hold students' interest. The teacher can stand next to one box, point, and say, "This box is blue" and "That box is blue." This sets up a minimal pair: the only distinction between the two objects is their proximity to the teacher. As soon as students seem to catch on, the teacher can move to the other box and say, "This box is blue," thus showing that the demonstrative changes according to the referent's distance from the speaker. Two sets of boxes can be used for *these boxes* and *those boxes*. Each point can be underscored by writing it on the board, by inviting different students to take the place of the teacher, and finally by allowing students to practice in pairs, placing objects close to and far from themselves. If students already know the names of colors and various objects, it is not necessary to limit realia too strictly, but don't overload students cognitively. They should focus on form rather than wrestle with lexicon.

Name the Objects

Realia can also be used in the communicative practice phase of a grammar lesson. The following exercise for practicing attributive adjectives and their order is based on a suggestion from Tim Butterworth and Darlene Schultz, who exploit an old baby shower game.[1] Place a number of small objects, each of which can be described by more than one adjective, on a table. This exercise is particularly challenging if you include items that differ in only one attribute, such as a small gold cuff link and a small silver cuff link. Allow students to study the objects

---

[1] Reported in Celce-Murcia and Larsen Freeman (1983: 399).

for a few minutes, and clarify the names of any objects if necessary. Then cover the items with a cloth and have students divide into groups to recall as many items as possible. Instruct the groups to use attributive adjectives in describing them. A point is given for listing the item. A point is also given for each correct adjective in the correct position. Therefore, only one point would be given to a student who answers, "a cuff link" or "one pen red." In the first case, only the noun is provided; in the second, the adjective is provided, but in the wrong position. Therefore, only one point is given in each case. However, three points would be given for "a small, gold cuff link"—two for the adjectives in the correct position and one for the noun. Have each group write its list on an overhead transparency and let the class score each list to reinforce the exercise. The group with the most points wins.

Indirect Objects

Another effective use of realia is to present and practice indirect objects and indirect object movement. In this case there is a match between structure and discourse, and the technique used is storytelling. Have several items on hand, including a set of keys and a ball. Begin by throwing the ball up in the air. Elicit from the class what you have done (e.g., "You threw the ball in the air and caught it"). Write the sentence on the board. Then throw the ball to a student and elicit from the class, "You threw the ball to José." Write this sentence on the board as well. Then change the focus to *ball* by displaying several different things you could throw. Select an object, show it to the class, and then throw it to José. Ask the class, "What did I throw to José?" You want to elicit indirect movement (e.g., *You threw him the eraser*). It is important to remember that the two sentences, with and without indirect object movement, are not synonymous. Indirect object movement is pragmatically motivated, and teaching *I gave the book to Mary* and *I gave her the book* as synonymous could mislead students.

It is unnecessary to go into the details of discourse pragmatics with students unless they are quite advanced. Simply provide an appropriate situation for each sentence and practice it in that context. When the sentence with indirect object movement is on the board as well, let students examine the two forms and tell you what the difference is. Then go to four or five students and ask them to take an object out

of their purse or pocket. Make sure each student takes out a differen
object. Try to get a set of keys or something else that requires a plural
pronoun among the objects. Collect the objects and bring them to the
front of the room. Hold up one and ask the class, "Whose compact
is this?" The class will answer, "It's Maria's." Then ask the class,
"Should I give Maria a pencil?" Point to the compact and shake your
head so students will say, "No! Give her the compact!" This will produce a natural situation in which we have indirect object movement.
Go through the same routine with a couple of other objects and then
invite a student to take over your role.

As each sentence is elicited, write it on the board. Draw students'
attention to the fact that the name of the person you are giving something
to can come before the name of the object being given. You want them
also to discover that when this occurs, the preposition is deleted. Once
the class has uncovered the pattern and seems to understand it, divide
the class into groups. Have each member of the group take out an object and put it in a pile in the middle of the group. Then one student
in each group picks up an object (not his own) while his group gives
directions as to its disposition. Walk around and listen to each group.
Answer questions or intervene as necessary.

USING THE CLASSROOM

Not all teachers have the budget, time, or inclination to prepare props
for the types of exercises described above. However, the classroom
itself provides a wealth of realia to use in teaching grammar. Ordinary
items found in most classrooms, such as books, tables, chairs, a flag,
a light switch, windows, walls, and the ceiling, can all be used. Let
us consider several structures and how they might be presented or practiced using the classroom.

Phrasal Verbs

The classroom provides a natural context for teaching phrasal verbs
such as *turn on* and *turn off*. The teacher can turn on a light and turn
it off, and then invite a student to come to the light switch and do the
same, using the TPR technique discussed in Chapter Three.

The students are also part of the classroom environment and

commands *sit down* and *stand up* or *take off* and *put* of clothing they all have, such as a jacket or coat. Students ited to give the commands as soon as possible. It has been ce that it is easy to underestimate how long it takes to learn of verbs. A great deal of time may be required to internalize the difference between turning a radio up, down, on, or off. We also suggest that teachers do only a few commands at a time, two or three times a week for about fifteen minutes during class, and repeat and review at regular intervals.

One final bit of advice regarding phrasal verbs. Whenever the phrasal verb is separable, make sure that some of your directions illustrate this by using the commands in both ways: *Take off the coat* as well as *Take it off.*

Prepositions

The people and the ordinary objects found in most classrooms can be of great assistance in presenting and practicing prepositions. For example, to present locative prepositions, one can use a table, a pencil, a book, a box, and a pen for structured practice of the difference between *in* and *on*. First the teacher puts the pen on the table and asks, "Where's the pen?" to which the class responds, "on the table." Then the teacher puts the pencil in the box and asks, "Where's the pencil?" to which the class responds, "in the box." This practice continues as the teacher manipulates the objects to elicit *on the box*, *in the box*, *on the table*, etc. When the class is responding quickly and accurately to all the combinations possible, one of the students should come up, manipulate the objects, and ask fellow students, "Where's the pen (book/box/pencil/etc.)?"

A more advanced version of the TPR method mentioned in Chapter Three takes advantage of the classroom and students for the presentation phase or structured practice portion of a lesson on reduced relative clauses: using a classroom set of texts (all of which look alike), the teacher places one book under the chair, one book on the chair, one book beside the chair, and so on around the room. Then she asks a student to come to the front of the room, where he is given the following commands:

"Touch the book under the table. Pick up the book beside the chair and put it on the chair. Pick up the book on the chair and put it on top of the book in the drawer."

You can even combine TPR with storytelling and roleplay for structured practice of locative prepositions, as in:

"José has five dollars that he wants to hide from Maria. Somebody tell him where to put the money so Maria won't find it."

Allow the class to give José suggestions, such as "Put it in the drawer" or "Put it under the book." As students learn prepositions of location, you can expand the list to encourage other uses of prepositions. For example, to encourage more advanced students to use the proxy *for*, you can say:

"Tom, Mary wants to open the door, but she is carrying too many books. Show us your books, Mary. You poor thing! Tom, help Mary. Open the door *for* her."

Like practice with phrasal verbs, these types of exercises can be carried out for a few minutes at the beginning of each class period after they have been introduced. Use commands to which all students can respond at the same time, such as:

"Pick up your pen. Put it on your notebook. Put it under your chair. Put it on your neighbor's desk. Put your book next to your pen. Now, put everything back on your desk. Look up. Look at me. Let's get started with today's lesson."

This activity is a good way to begin each class. It can be used to review the previous day's lesson while not requiring a special group of students in front of the class or any special supplies.

Relative Clauses

One of the most difficult aspects of teaching relative clauses is providing sufficient context to justify their use. We have found an effective way to do this in the presentation phase of the lesson by using students and the classroom. Call two students to the front of the room who are of the same sex. Have one sit down and the other stand a few yards away. Then announce to the class that you are going to give the eraser to the woman who is standing up. Then ask students to identify which of their colleagues you are going to give the eraser to. The class will respond, "Maria!" or "Kiko!" When they have responded cor-

rectly, give the eraser to the woman who is standing. Then pick up
a book and go through the entire routine again. Call two different
students to the front of the class and continue the routine. When the
class as a whole is responding correctly, call up a student and ask him
to give the orders. You can then move from those very concrete relative
clauses to more abstract ones. Ask the two students in front of the room,
"Where are you from?" "What is your favorite food?" "Are you
married?" "Do you want to get married?" Then ask a student to give
the book to "the man who is from Cambodia" or "the girl who likes
ice cream."

    To present center-embedded relative clauses (i.e., relative clauses
that modify the subject), you can use a variation of the old "Button,
Button" game. Use pennies instead of buttons, if you want, since
pennies are readily available in the classroom. Invite several students
of the same sex to the front of the room. Ask the class to question them
so they will have enough information to form relative clauses. As the
class elicits information, write several phrases about each student behind
them on the board. For example, behind one student you might write
the following in response to your questions:
- has never seen a movie star
- likes ice cream
- is looking for a job

After you have written several phrases behind each student, hold a
penny up for the whole class to see, and then put it between your hands.
Have the students in front of the room hold out their hands, palms
together at a 45-degree angle. Put your hands between each student's
hands and have them close them immediately after you remove yours.
Secretly deposit the penny in the hands of one of the students. Then
ask the class, "Which person has the penny?" Students have to provide the answer using an embedded relative clause (e.g., "The woman
who has never seen a movie star has the penny."). Whenever a correct
form is elicited, write it on the board, even if it doesn't fit the student
who has the penny. Continue until students discover who has the penny.
Perhaps they will guess correctly, or perhaps you will have to respond,
"No, it's the woman who's looking for a job!" Then review all sentences
you've written on the board and let the class make relative clauses with
the phrases that were not used. If you keep things moving fast, students

will be interested. They will see that relative clauses can distinguish between individual members of a set, and they will be able to practice the form as well.

CONCLUSION

In this chapter we have suggested that realia and objects in the classroom are vital teaching aids, particularly for grammar points which have a structure-meaning match. We have suggested that realia be used in conjunction with storytelling and roleplay techniques to contextualize the grammar lesson, as well as facilitate memory and learning. A set of realia can be gathered from children's toy boxes, garage sales, and thrift stores, but virtually all classrooms come equipped with resources that we tend to overlook, not the least of which is the students themselves. We have also suggested that realia, under a broad definition, can facilitate the learning of grammar, in addition to the more familiar role it plays in the learning of vocabulary.

·ACTIVITIES·

Discussion Questions

1. Do you agree that in teaching a second language, the use of realia (under our broad definition) correlates with Barbara Schumann's pedagogical suggestions? Why or why not?

2. Do you feel that realia could be an effective resource for teaching grammar? Why or why not?

3. Look around you right now as you read this question. Identify at least five objects or people you could use as realia to teach a grammar lesson. What would the grammar objectives be?

4. What are the drawbacks to using realia? Do they outweigh the advantages as you see them?

Suggested Activities

1. Make a list of items around the house which could be useful in your ESL classes. Then collect those items and bring them in to show your colleagues, specifying the grammar points you would teach using them.

2. Plan a grammar lesson using some of the props you have collected and try it out on your colleagues. Ask them to do the same so you have a chance to both give and get a lesson using realia. Review the lesson from both the perspective of the teacher and the students, and amend the lesson accordingly.

3. Consider a fairly complex piece of realia, such as a small child's tricycle. List grammatical structure(s) that could be taught effectively using this piece of realia in the classroom [e.g., comparatives (*bigger than, smaller than*), plurals (*one wheel, three wheels*), or logical connectors (*and then, after that*)]. The possibilities are virtually limitless, once you begin. Give yourself some time and you will find this exercise very helpful.

GRAPHICS

This chapter shows how to use charts, tables, schedules, graphs, and other graphic aids as resources to facilitate both focused and communicative practice of grammar. In general, intermediate and advanced students are the intended audience for such exercises; however, some of the graphics can be simplified for use with sophisticated beginners. Graphics are not only useful in developing communicative activities, but are also natural resources for practicing a variety of structures. These teaching aids, which primarily encourage the learner to make a form-meaning match, may also involve texts as part of the activity and in such cases will help the learner make a form-discourse match, too.

The use of graphics as a resource to teach ESL students was a proposal specifically advanced by Shaw and Taylor (1978), who referred to such aids as "non-pictorial visuals." As a general trend, virtually all reference books dealing with the communicative approach to language teaching (e.g., Littlewood 1981, Johnson and Morrow 1981, among others) and all teaching materials based on the communicative approach make use of graphic aids because stimuli such as charts, tables, graphs, and schedules lend themselves well to the development of communicative tasks.

CHARTS AND TABLES

Charts and tables are helpful teaching tools, usable at even the lowest level if the teacher focuses on students themselves rather than on technical information that involves a lot of numbers or statistics.

If students are in college and come from many different countries, a class chart like the one below can be used in completed form to encourage more advanced students to practice constructing extended texts using logical connectors of comparison and contrast. (Of course, the students would already have been introduced to the use of *and*, *but*, *while/whereas*, and relative clauses):

Student Name	Native Country	Native Language	Major Field of Study	Interest(s)	Students' Choice
Hamid Ali	Egypt	Arabic	Engineering	Photography	
Mario Campos	Mexico	Spanish	Business	Archaeology	
Peter Hwang	Korea	Korean	Chemistry	Volleyball	
Kenji Kawamoto	Japan	Japanese	Engineering	Jazz	
Carlos Muñoz	Mexico	Spanish	Physical Education	Soccer	

Texts like the following have been generated during the classwork:
"Hamid Ali and Kenji Kawamoto both study engineering, but Hamid likes photography while Kenji enjoys jazz (or, but Hamid comes from Egypt, whereas Kenji is from Japan)."
If, on the other hand, the class contains secondary-level, college-level, or private-language school students, and if all come from the same country or town, the class chart can be modified to include categories such as these:

- occupation
- interests/hobbies
- reason(s) for studying English
- marital status
- personality type (outgoing, shy, logical, etc.)
- favorite vacation spot
- favorite food
- favorite color

The teacher should know or find out what categories will work best for her class. Students should also be allowed to add one category of their own to a class chart. Our students have chosen categories as diverse as marital status, age, number and sex of siblings, and first impressions of the United States.

For focused practice of relative clauses of identification with

existential *there*, the teacher can prepare two versions of the chart, one
that contains all the information and the names in alphabetical order,
the other without names and with the other information for each student intact but in random order. Students work in pairs—each with
a different list— but do not see each other's charts. The teacher then
indicates that the student who has no names should begin by saying
something like this:

> S1: There's a student in our class who comes from Mexico and
> who studies physical education . . .

From the description provided by Student 1, Student 2 should be able
to find the name on his list:

> S2: Oh, I see! It's Carlos Muñoz.
> S1: Who?
> S2: Carlos Muñoz. (Spell out the name if necessary.)
> C-A-R-L-O-S M-U-Ñ-O-Z.

This procedure continues until Student 1 has filled in all the names
in the empty name column on his chart. The activity becomes amusing when the name turns out to be that of one of the students in the pair.

Many ESL students are avid sports fans, and sports information can provide a good basis for charts. Statistics that appear in the
sports sections of newspapers, for example, can be incorporated in a
chart and thus be used for communicative grammar practice of a form-
meaning match. The following baseball chart, taken from *The Christian
Science Monitor*, lends itself to communicative practice of *wh*-questions
with *which*, superlatives, and logical connectors of reason:

U.S. Major League Baseball
Standings and Statistics
through games of Sept. 25

NATIONAL LEAGUE

Eastern Division	W	L	Pct.	GB	Western Division	W	L	Pct.	GB
St. Louis	96	56	.632	—	Los Angeles	89	63	.586	—
New York	92	60	.605	4	Cincinnati	82	68	.547	6
Montreal	79	73	.520	17	Houston	78	74	.513	11
Philadelphia	71	79	.473	24	San Diego	77	75	.507	12
Chicago	71	80	.470	24½	Atlanta	62	89	.411	26½
Pittsburgh	52	98	.347	43	San Francisco	59	93	.388	30

AMERICAN LEAGUE

Eastern Division					Western Division				
	W	L	Pct.	GB		W	L	Pct.	GB
Toronto	95	56	.629	—	California	86	66	.566	—
New York	89	62	.589	6	Kansas City	85	66	.563	½
Baltimore	79	71	.527	15½	Chicago	78	73	.517	7½
Detroit	79	73	.520	16½	Oakland	74	78	.487	12
Boston	76	76	.500	19½	Seattle	71	81	.467	15
Milwaukee	67	84	.444	28	Minnesota	70	82	.461	16
Cleveland	55	99	.357	41½	Texas	57	94	.377	28½

In this activity students work in pairs but do not see each other's handout. (The teacher should try to pair someone who knows little or nothing about the sport with someone who is very knowledgeable.) One student has the above chart and the other has a sheet that looks like this:

Highs and Lows of Major League Baseball
through Sept. 25

Team	Answer	Reason
1. best percentage		
2. worst percentage		
3. most games behind		
4. most games ahead		
Division		
1. the closest race		
2. the least interesting race		

The object is for the student with the answer/reason chart to interview the one with the standings and statistics chart to get the necessary information. It is a good idea to give students a model like the following dialog, so they know what's expected:

S1:   Which team has the best percentage?

S2:   St. Louis.

S1:   How do you know?

S2:   Because St. Louis has a percentage of .632 and Toronto, the next closest team, has a percentage of .629.

Another chart-type exercise allows the teacher to exploit Fahrenheit and Centigrade temperature-scale differences by preparing two news clippings containing the temperatures for major cities of the world on a given day of the year. One clipping has the temperature in Fahrenheit degrees from the *New York Times*, the second in Centigrade degrees from *Le Monde*, a Paris newspaper. Both clippings are from December 24, and the teacher explains that both have some temperature readings that are illegible or blank because of problems in the printing process. A third piece of information available to each pair or group are the formulas for converting Fahrenheit into Centigrade or vice versa.

Conversion formulas
Centigrade degrees ÷ 5, × 9, + 32 = Fahrenheit degrees
Fahrenheit degrees − 32, ÷ 9, × 5 = Centigrade degrees

The task of each pair or small group (there should be at least one student with good basic math skills in each group) is to reconstruct the missing information in each clipping.

Clipping 1		Clipping 2	
New York Times		*Le Monde*	
(Fahrenheit degrees)		(Centigrade degrees)	
Buenos Aires	☐	Buenos Aires	30
Cairo	68	Le Caire	☐
London	42	Londres	☐
Madrid	☐	Madrid	09
Moscow	− 04	Moscou	− 20
New York	32	New York	☐
Paris	50	Paris	10
Tokyo	☐	Tokyo	08

The structures given communicative practice here are the singular subject-verb agreement used in mathematical addition, subtraction, multiplication, and division:

 2 plus 2 equals 4.
 4 minus 2 equals 2.
 2 times 2 equals 4.
 4 divided by 2 equals 2.

The exercise also allows for focus on the passive voice for multiplication (optional) and division (obligatory):

 2 times 2 equals 4 or 2 *multiplied by* 2 equals 4.
 4 *divided by* 2 equals 2.

   To help the students complete this exercise the teacher should do several things: first, warn students that the names of cities are sometimes spelled differently in English and French, but that they are usually similar enough to match; second, walk the class through the formulas using two cities not cited on the exercise clippings; third, pause after every occurrence of equals and encourage the class to complete the formula at that time. The class should repeat the wording of each step as the conversion evolves. The exercise, then, would proceed something like this:

   T: On December 24, it was 72 degrees Fahrenheit in New Delhi. To figure out the Centigrade equivalent, we apply the formula this way:
   • Step 1: 72 minus 32 equals . . . 40.
   • Step 2: 40 divided by 9 equals . . . 4.44.
   • Step 3: 4.44 multiplied by 5 equals . . . 22.2.
   Conclusion: Therefore we know it was 22 degrees Centigrade
        in New Delhi on December 24.

   On December 24, it was 13.5 Centigrade in Athens. To figure out the Fahrenheit equivalent, we apply the formula this way:
   • Step 1: 13.5 divided by 5 equals . . . 2.7.
   • Step 2: 2.7 multiplied by 9 equals . . . 24.3.
   • Step 3: 24.3 plus 32 equals . . . 56.3.
   Conclusion: Therefore we know it was 56 degrees Fahrenheit
        in Athens on December 24.
Students should be encouraged to verbalize the steps of each conversion as they do their work in pairs or groups. Use of calculators is encouraged, especially if there is a disagreement about the correct answer.

   Once everyone has completed the six conversions, one pair or group should put its answers on the board so the other groups will have a chance to agree or disagree with the results. The correct answers are:

   New York Times: Buenos Aires 86, Madrid 48, Tokyo 46
   Le Monde: Le Caire 20, Londres 12, New York 0

   If appropriate, the completed charts can be used to quickly review comparative and superlative constructions. For example:

On December 24, the (*coldest/warmest*) city was _____.

City X was (*colder/warmer*) than city Y on December 24.

Teachers should adapt the clippings used in such an exercise so cities of special interest to students in their classes can be included.

SCHEDULES

Printed schedules for planes, trains, buses, and boats are rich sources of data for focused grammar exercises based on graphic resources. We will give one illustration of such an exercise using information from a timetable for the Route #3 bus line in Santa Monica, California, as our source of data. The #3 line runs between the Los Angeles International Airport (LAX) and UCLA. There are several points of interest along the route: Marina del Rey (Fiji Way), Venice, Ocean Park, Santa Monica Mall, and the West Los Angeles Veterans Hospital. A partial bus schedule for the early morning hours provides the following information about travel time between LAX and UCLA and the various points of interest in between:

LAX	Mar. del Rey	Venice	Ocean Park	S.M. Mall	WLA VA Hosp.	UCLA
A.M.						
6:50	7:05	7:12	7:20	7:29	7:48	7:59
7:30	7:45	7:52	8:00	8:09	8:28	8:39
8:05	8:20	8:27	8:35	8:44	9:03	9:14
8:45	9:00	9:07	9:15	9:24	9:43	9:54
9:25	9:40	9:47	9:55	10:04	10:23	10:34
10:05	10:20	10:27	10:35	10:44	11:03	11:14

This information provides a context for either focused or communicative practice of prepositions of location and orientation:

from . . . to

"On bus #3 you can travel from (point X) to (point Y)."

between

"On bus #3 you can travel between (point X) and (point Y).

The use of *at* referring to a specific geographical point or to a point in time can also be practiced:

"The 6:50 LAX bus arrives *at* (point X) at (time Y)."

Another obvious construction for practice is the use of *wh*-questions of duration (i.e., *how long*):

"How long does it take to travel from (point X) to (point Y)?"

Travel schedules also lend themselves to focused practice of the adjectival use of the present participle in a fill-in-the-blanks exercise:

"The bus _____ from LAX at (time X) will arrive at UCLA at (time Y)."

A variety of participle forms such as *leaving*, *departing*, and *starting* are all acceptable in such an exercise. Lexical variety should, in fact, be encouraged. This resource can also be used for focused practice in expressing the future with the present tense:

"The bus arriving at UCLA at 10:34 tomorrow morning _____ LAX at _____."

In addition, the schedule above might also be used to practice future conditional questions to elicit different kinds of temporal information:

Duration: "If you want to go from (point X) to (point Y), how long will it take?"

Arrival time: "If you leave (point X) at (time Y), when will you arrive at (point Z)?

GRAPHS

One of the most common uses of line graphs is to show trends, or ups and downs, over a period of time. The lines in these graphs approximate numerical values or percentages in contrast to tables or charts, where numbers give very precise information. Before students are presented with a line graph, such as the one below, the teacher should present a general review of the topic by asking the following questions:

- How often do presidential elections take place in the United States?
- When was the last election year?
- When will the next presidential election take place?
- Who was elected in each presidential election since 1960?

At this point, the teacher can present the graph to the class, along with a few questions that will encourage interpretation:

- What do the numbers, which appear going from left to right along the bottom of the graph, represent?
- What does the left vertical bar represent?
- What does it mean when the black line goes up/down?

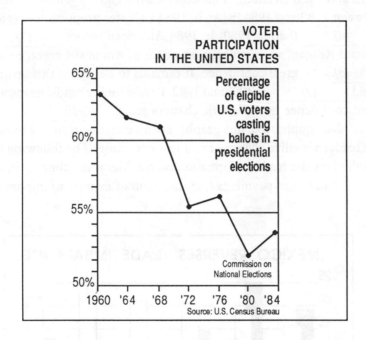

Once there is a general understanding of the graph, students can be given the following structured exercise: a modified cloze passage based on the graph and designed to practice sequence of tenses. In this particular passage students have to use the present perfect, the simple past, the simple present (optionally), and the simple future. Leaving the lexical choice up to students (as we have done) makes the exercise more demanding. For less advanced students, you may wish to list possible verbs on the chalkboard or at the bottom of the cloze passage. Also, you may well have to clarify some of the other vocabulary in the passage. Students can do this exercise individually and then compare their answers working in pairs or small groups:

According to data from the U.S. Census Bureau and the Commission on National Elections, voter participation in presidential elections   _(1)_   since 1960. The two steepest declines   _(2)_   between 1968 and 1972 and between 1976 and 1980. Even though Richard Nixon   _(3)_   the election in 1972, voters   _(4)_   strong disillusionment with an incumbent president before both the 1972 and 1980 elections. This downward trend   _(5)_   itself between 1980 and 1984, when in 1984 a greater proportion of voters   _(6)_   than in 1980. In 1984 American voters   _(7)_   Ronald Reagan, an incumbent president in whom the average voter   _(8)_   great confidence. It remains to be seen if this upward trend   _(9)_   in 1988 and 1992. If the winning candidate inspires great confidence in the voters, chances are it   _10_   .

Bar graphs, like line graphs, are an effective resource to help the reader visualize change or contrast over time. The following bar graph gives the reader information on the Mexican economy in the area of balance of payments (i.e., the ratio of exports to imports).

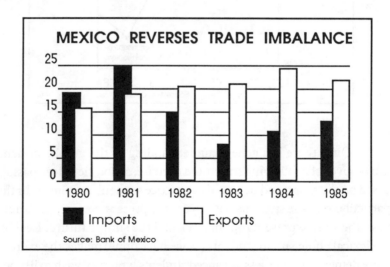

For this graph, the teacher should provide background by discussing the topic and special vocabulary such as *imports, exports, balance of payments, trade imbalance, rise, exceed, decline,* and *reverse.*

Once this has been accomplished, the bar graph can be presented to students for interpretation:

- What do the numbers going up the left, 0 to 25, represent?
- Why are there two bars for each year, a gray one and a black one?

When students understand the graph, they should work in pairs to complete the following worksheet, which gives them focused practice in distinguishing simple past and present perfect *vis a vis* trends or states that are completed in the past (signalled by the simple past), as opposed to trends or states that continue into the present (signalled by the present perfect).

1. In 1980 imports _____ exports by four billion dollars.
2. Imports _____ exports in 1980 and 1981.
3. Exports _____ imports since 1982.
4. Exports _____ imports in 1982, 1983, 1984, and 1985.
5. The trade imbalance _____ in 1982.
6. Since 1983 exports _____ imports by more than ten billion dollars.
7. From 1981 to 1983 exports _____*(a)*_____ , but since 1983 they _____*(b)*_____ .

After the class works together to share and correct answers on the worksheet, students (individually or in pairs) should write a paragraph about balance of payments in Mexico between 1980 and 1985 with attention to correct use of the simple past and present perfect.

IMAGINATIVE USES OF GRAPHICS

Most of the preceding activities exploiting graphic aids have been rather information-based and academic in nature. These teaching aids, however, also can be used for humorous or amusing activities, while still allowing for grammar practice. We therefore conclude our discussion with two activities on the lighter side. One provides communicative practice of *wh*-questions and complex *yes/no* questions with *that* complements, while the other provides practice in comprehending negative *yes/no* questions.

As background for the first activity, the teacher will have to provide a list of the twelve signs of the zodiac, along with the birth dates ruled by the signs, and one or two of the dominant personality traits that supposedly correspond to each sign. This information is provided on the following worksheet, which will be used as the basis for the activity:

Sign (constellation)	Dates	Trait	Names of Classmates	Notes on Traits
Capricorn (goat)	Dec. 22–Jan. 19	dedicated, tireless		
Aquarius (water carrier)	Jan. 20–Feb. 18	dynamic, colorful		
Pisces (fish)	Feb. 19–Mar. 20	meditative, compassionate		
Aries (ram)	Mar. 21–Apr. 19	strong willed, enthusiastic		
Taurus (bull)	Apr. 20–May 20	graceful, wise		
Gemini (twins)	May 21–June 20	cheerful, energetic		
Cancer (crab)	June 21–July 22	sensitive, sincere		
Leo (lion)	July 23–Aug. 22	charming, clever		
Virgo (virgin)	Aug. 23–Sept. 22	decisive, upright		
Libra (balance)	Sept. 23–Oct. 22	intelligent, loyal		
Scorpio (scorpion)	Oct. 23–Nov. 21	resolute, diligent		
Sagittarius (archer)	Nov. 22–Dec. 21	forthright, honest		

Before distributing the chart, the teacher can warm up the clas
by asking if anyone believes in astrology. Usually a few students will
answer positively. Then the teacher can say, "I'm a _____
(sign)" and call on one of the students who expressed some belief in
astrology by asking, "What's your sign?" or "What are you?" Both
the teacher's and the students' signs can be written on the board; ask
the class to provide names of some other signs and discuss their
significance. The teacher must also ensure that students understand
all vocabulary in the "trait" column. After this brief warm-up, some
students who are unfamiliar with the Western-Middle Eastern-Indian
zodiac might want to know what their sign is, so this would be an appropriate time to distribute the handout.

Next, the teacher must decide on the optimal grouping and configuration for this activity. For example, if the class is small (fifteen
or fewer students) there can be one group. Larger classes should be
divided into two or more groups. If students in the class occasionally
act unruly, the groups should sit in large circles, with one student being
interviewed at a time. More mature students can circulate and interview
each other one-on-one.

The three tasks for each group (regardless of configuration) are:
1. Determine the sign of every person in your group.
2. As soon as you have elicited the sign, ask whether the person
   feels she exemplifies the trait(s) on the chart.
3. In more advanced classes, group members then work in pairs
   to write a paragraph summarizing the findings from the
   survey. It should end with a logical conclusion about the
   validity of the zodiac's predictions for group members (e.g.,
   Since ten of the twelve members in the group did not feel
   that the zodiac correctly predicted their personality traits,
   we can conclude . . .).

The first task requires simple *wh*-questions such as: "What's
your sign?" or "What are you?" whereas the second task elicits a complex question with a *that* complement typical of an interview context:
"Do you feel/think that you're loyal?" Students should also take notes
as they gather the information. Finally, the pairs of students in each
group should share or exchange their paragraphs to check for accuracy
of content (i.e., facts about the group), soundness of the conclusion,

and accuracy of form (i.e., grammar). This can be done very easily if students working in pairs write their paragraphs directly onto an acetate transparency for later projection to the class on an overhead projector.[1]

For the second whimsical activity, which affords a delightful way to introduce negative *yes/no* questions, the teacher needs nine photocopied pages of sheet music—or photocopied pages from a book— which should be taped up or pinned to the board in a three-by-three configuration. The pages, which should not contain illustrations or other idiosyncratic markings, can be more or less randomly selected from any piano anthology, novel, or textbook.

To carry out the activity the teacher needs an accomplice, preferably a good student, whom he has briefed in advance. The accomplice leaves the room or turns his back so he cannot see the board while a class volunteer comes to the front and secretly chooses one of the nine sheets. Let's say the volunteer picks the middle sheet in the center of the configuration.

The accomplice turns around or reenters the room, and the teacher points to any sheet and asks either, "Is it this one?" or "Isn't it this one?" being careful to keep the intonation as uniform as possible regardless of question form. The use of the affirmative *yes/no* question with its neutral expectation signals to the accomplice that the answer is "no." The use of a negative *yes/no* question, with its more strongly positive presupposition, signals to the accomplice that the teacher is pointing to the target sheet, and this form thus elicits "yes" from the accomplice. For variety, the teacher and accomplice may exchange roles while the procedure is being repeated. The teacher and accomplice should be careful to vary the number of times the questions are asked before the target sheet is identified.

The class's task, of course, is to figure out how the accomplice, or the teacher, knows with perfect accuracy which sheet has been secretly targeted. As soon as a student thinks she knows the "trick," she should try to be the accomplice. If she can pick out the target sheet three times in a row, the teacher can step back permanently and let

---

[1] For other ideas on how to use the zodiac for language practice, see Shaw and Taylor 1978.

the new student and the accomplice carry on and exchange roles until another student figures out the "trick." The rotation of new students into the task continues. Often students think they understand what is going on, but they do not, and this becomes apparent when they cannot identify the target sheet. (This is frequently a source of amusement to classmates.)

After several students have figured out what to do, then the "trick" and its linguistic basis can be explained to the remaining students. Allow the whole class a few minutes to practice the activity in small groups with an appropriate visual aid, such as nine playing cards on a desk, so the remaining students also have an opportunity to contrast the use of affirmative and negative *yes/no* questions in this context.

This activity helps learners to better comprehend the presuppositions of affirmative and negative *yes/no* questions in English, at least in this type of context, and is an entertaining presentation of this contrast.

CONCLUSION

When using graphic aids, ESL teachers should realize that not everyone can readily interpret such visuals. Initial proficiency depends partly on one's culture and level of education. These graphics are a very western concept. The activities presented are intended to be suggestive and illustrative, not exhaustive. Shaw and Taylor (1978) provide several other useful suggestions for incorporating graphic aids into language practice.

ESL textbooks are not necessarily the best source of visuals for these activities. Textbooks in economics, geography, psychology, sociology, and business usually contain many tables, charts, and graphs, some of which can be adapted for use in the ESL classroom. Such textbooks, of course, become even more relevant if your students happen to be studying one of these content areas. Certain newspapers and magazines are also good sources of graphics to adapt for language practice.

In the most authentic ESL teaching materials, graphics often accompany a written text. Thus, with intermediate and advanced students, it might be best to include the relevant text and to develop reading activities for comprehending the text, as well as oral activities for interpreting and discussing the graphic.

Using this type of resource in the ESL classroom becomes particularly urgent if your students are preparing for some competency-based exam, since these tests typically demand that the test-taker demonstrate an ability to interpret tables, charts, and graphs.

In any case, graphic aids are the analytic counterpart to the more holistic pictures we discussed earlier in Chapter Six. Both match form with meaning, and both can be very effective tools for teaching grammar. While pictures can be used for presentation, focused practice, and communicative practice, graphics are generally best suited for focused or communicative practice. However, as our last exercise suggests, they can also be used on occasion during the presentation phase. In addition, many of the activities involving graphics encourage a form-discourse match as well as a form-meaning match, since texts are often read or generated in the course of doing these exercises.

·ACTIVITIES·

Discussion Questions

1. What groups of language learners will benefit most/least from the use of graphic aids?

2. Would you use graphic aids to practice a grammatical structure(s)? If so, what structure(s)?

3. What are some good sources of graphic aids other than the ones mentioned in this chapter?

Suggested Activities

1. Examine some current ESL textbooks until you find one that uses a graphic aid to teach a structure. What is the graphic, the structure, and the task? Do you feel the proposed exercise is fully effective? If not, show how you would modify the exercise to increase its effectiveness.

2. Go through a newspaper or magazine. Find a graphic aid that can be used to teach a particular structure. Outline the way you would use the graphic to teach the structure. Share your idea with some colleages. What was their reaction?

·CHAPTER NINE·
Techniques and Resources Integrated

SONGS AND VERSE

The next three chapters deal with technique-resource combinations. These combinations are particularly suited to a structure-discourse match and can be used for virtually all phases of a grammar lesson. Let us begin by considering two enjoyable but nonetheless effective technique-resource combinations: songs and verse.

Music and poetry in an ESL class can give a fresh perspective on the language we are teaching. Through them, the language we have been dissecting into a series of structural points becomes whole again. It has been our experience that songs and poetry in the ESL classroom can revive our love and respect for English and can bring to mind again the joy and exquisite beauty of the language we have chosen to teach, in a way that many of us have long forgotten.

SONGS

As we have suggested before, contextualization is essential to any grammar presentation and meaningful practice of structure, and certainly one of the most delightful and culturally rich resources for contextualization is song. Dubin (1974) points out that, "Songs can be utilized as presentation contexts, as reinforcement material, as vehicles through which to teach all language skills, and as a medium through which to present some of the most important cultural themes which pervade modern life."[1]

[1] Paper presented at the TESOL Convention, Denver, CO, on March 7, 1974, cited in Pomeroy (1974).

Hulquist (1984), in an unpublished handbook of activities for adult ESL students, suggests that songs—in conjunction with other grammar presentation activities—can be effective in five different ways by:

1. adding variety as well as enjoyment to language learning (all skills)
2. presenting authentic language, as well as introducing students to various dialects spoken in the United States
3. allowing students to practice a previously studied, contrasting structure along with a new structure
4. providing an opportunity to apply language skills to real-life situations by extending the pattern in the song
5. helping to develop cultural awareness, both of the present and the past

Pomeroy (1974) maintains that, "There is indeed an American music, a music which reveals and reflects the culture of the American people. By looking at the kind of songs Americans sing and the periods in which they sang them, we can see that the songs reflect the mood of the time. This can help us to understand the Americans themselves" (p. 6). Further, Pomeroy says that the repetition that naturally occurs in songs can make drill work easier and more pleasant (p. 21) and points out that songs which contain repetition or substitution can be helpful in teaching and expanding grammatical patterns. In fact, Kind (1980) has developed an entire beginning language-learning method based wholly on songs. Kind's method is used for teaching German, French, and Spanish, as well as English.

In spite of these recommendations, many ESL and EFL teachers are reluctant to use songs in the classroom, quite possibly because they consider them frivolous or unproductive. Moreover, they fear (and often rightly so) that their students will have a similar opinion. The social aspect of an adult school is very important to mature learners; however, we should be careful not to confuse the importance of this aspect with the reason why adults attend ESL classes. They come primarily to learn English, not just to have fun. No matter how clever or entertaining the teacher, students can always have more fun at home with their families and friends. Of course, affective factors are vitally important in ESL classes (see Conclusion), but affect contributes to learning—it does not substitute for it— and students come to class because they feel they are learning something. Conversely, if students feel they are not learning, they do not come to school. Teachers who have experienced this may be concerned that students will view singing songs as an unprofessional attempt at "fun" rather than an effective learning context, and therefore avoid music in their lessons. The concern is well-founded, unless students are informed ahead of time precisely why they are singing and what the teacher expects to accomplish with a musical component in the language lesson.

According to Gasser and Waldman (1979), songs provide an enjoyable way to introduce or review vocabulary and idiomatic expressions, teach pronunciation, introduce various aspects of American culture, and present or review structures and sentence patterns in a novel way. Songs provide a context for interesting and effective focused grammar practice, but we suggest that before beginning a lesson that includes songs, teachers make the benefits clear to students. For example, the teacher could explain, "We are going to practice the present perfect as well as learn a few idioms with this song. We are also going to work on pronunciation." A straightforward explanation often goes a long way toward enlisting the participation of students.

Selection Guidelines

Songs for use in the ESL classroom must be selected with care. For example, Pomeroy humorously points out that teaching "Jingle Bells" will allow students to practice *upsot* as the past participle of *upset*, and "We three kings of Orient, are" gives practice in producing sentences with a verb final construction. In fact, according to Pomeroy, many songs stress words or even syllables which ordinarily do not receive stress.

Both Pomeroy and Gasser and Waldman provide guidelines for selecting songs. The following list is a synthesis of their suggestions:

1. Songs must be of a singable length, range, and rhythm. Verses should be short, and melodies should have a one-octave range and an uncomplicated rhythmic pattern.
2. Songs should have repetitive lyrics or a chorus which is easy to learn. This allows even the slowest students to participate.
3. Lyrics should reflect standard spoken English, with respect to register, subject-verb agreement, and word order. As

Gasser and Waldman point out, " 'Greensleeves' is a lovely melody but no one today would actually say, 'Alas, my
love, you do me wrong, to cast me off so discourteously' "
(p. 50).

4. The emotional and conceptual content of a song should be
appropriate to the age and maturity of the students.

5. Songs must be pedagogically appropriate to the teaching
point, and not so colloquial as to require that the lyrics be
changed into standard English.

Teaching Procedure

Gasser and Waldman suggest the following procedure for using songs
in the classroom:

1. Begin by introducing the song. Tell a little about it, the period
of American history during which it was written, who wrote
it, etc.[2]

2. Make the lyrics available to students, either by writing them
on the board for students to copy, handing out mimeographed
copies of the words, or providing lyrics with key words or
structures missing (a modified cloze exercise) that students
must listen for and fill in. This provides recognition practice as well.

3. Sing or play the song once and allow students to listen and
enjoy it. It's not necessary to be a competent singer yourself.
You can play a recording of the song, ask a musically talented
student to prepare ahead of time and perform the song, use
a videotape, or play a musical instrument.

4. Go through the lyrics with students aloud and check comprehension, understanding of lexical items, etc.

5. Go through the song one verse at a time, letting students
listen before they sing. If there is a chorus, let students practice it first.

6. Sing the entire song with the class several times. Once or
twice is not enough. Give students ample opportunity to prac-

---

[2] Cf. Pomeroy for a review of the different periods of American history and the songs
that reflect them.

tice, and remember that they are dealing with a tune, rhythm, and language all at once.

Example Songs

Now let's consider some specific examples of songs to use for particular grammar points.[3] Hulquist suggests the song "Gonna Build a Mountain" by Leslie Bricusse and Anthony Newley, from the musical production *Stop the World—I Want to Get Off* to practice future tense with *be* + *going to* and *will* + *verb*. The story is about a man who feels very sad and depressed about his life and wonders if it is worth living. By the end of the play, when the song is sung, he begins to have hope for a better life:

Gonna Build a Mountain

Gonna build a mountain, from a little hill.
Gonna build a mountain, 'least I hope I will.
Gonna build a mountain, gonna build it high.
I don't know how I'm gonna do it
     Only know I'm gonna try.

Gonna build a daydream, from a little hope.
Gonna push that daydream, up the mountain slope.
Gonna build a daydream. Gonna see it through.
Gonna build a mountain, and a daydream
     Gonna make 'em both come true.

Gonna build a heaven, from a little hell.
Gonna build a heaven, and I know darn well,
If I build my mountain with a lot of care,
And take my daydream up the mountain,
     Heaven will be waiting there.

---

[3] For an extensive list of songs, words, music, and grammar points, see Gasser and Waldman, Hulquist, Kind, Osman and McConochie (1979), Pomeroy, Richards (1969), Richards and Poliquin (1972), Shaw (1970), and *English Teaching Forum* (Winter 1966).

When I've built that heaven, as I will some day,
And the Lord sends Gabriel, to take me away,
Wanna fine young son to take my place.
I'll leave a son in my heaven on earth
                     With the Lord's good grace.

One of the most obvious things that must be called to students'
attention is that *gonna* is a reduced phonological form; it is spoken,
seldom written. Hulquist points out that one will see it occasionally
in comic strips, novels, and plays. Among the vocabulary items to
discuss ahead of time are *heaven*, *hell*, *darn*, and *grace*, as well as the
cultural significance of *Gabriel* and *the Lord*.

To practice the past progressive, Hulquist suggests "Surprise
Party," a song with lyrics by Uwe Kind and music of "Ode to Joy"
by Ludwig van Beethoven. The song is about a birthday party given
to a boy named Larry by his friends, who sneak into his apartment
with a birthday cake and wait for him to come home. Larry decides
to come home late, so his friends tire of waiting and begin the party
without him.

Surprise Party

When I reached my house at seven,
Max was playing the guitar.
Jane was sitting on the table
eating pickles from a jar.

Mark was sitting at the piano
playing sonatas for Louise,
and my parrot Paul was singing
all the tunes and melodies.

Bob was sleeping under the table;
he couldn't even stay awake.
And my dog was in the kitchen
eating up the birthday cake.

(From Uwe Kind's *Tune in to English*,
New York: Regents 1980)

To practice the present perfect, Hulquist suggests Woody Guthrie's "So Long, It's Been Good to Know Yuh" ("I've sung this song, but I'll sing it again/Of the people I've met and the places I've been") or Pete Seeger's "Where Have All the Flowers Gone?" Present perfect progressive can be practiced with "I've Been Working on the Railroad," and to practice reflexive pronouns you might use "Consider Yourself at Home" from the play and film *Oliver*.

Pomeroy suggests "A Little Help From My Friends," by John Lennon and Paul McCartney, to practice *wh*-questions, *somebody* and *anybody*, and phrasal verbs (*stand up*, *walk out*, *get by*); "Anything You Can Do, I Can Do Better," by Irving Berlin, for practicing comparatives; "If I Had a Hammer" for hypothetical conditionals; "I Could Have Danced All Night," by Alan Jay Lerner and Frederick Loewe, for past unreal conditionals; and "My Father," by Judy Collins, for contrasting the habitual use of the simple present and simple past.

Of course, you can make up your own lyrics for popular tunes students are familiar with.[4] Being alert to songs you hear every day, particularly songs from the 1960s, Broadway musicals, and contemporary hits, will provide you with more than enough interesting and adaptable material.

POETRY

Another interesting way to contextualize a grammar lesson is through poetry. Povey (1979) points out that "one of the most difficult things about teaching poetry to foreign students is handling the teacher's own deeply wrought unhappiness with verse, the result of experiences he or she has suffered" (p. 164). Indeed, many of us fear that our own attempts to teach poetry to our students will be met with the same sniggers and lack of cooperation that plagued our high school teachers; however, such behavior has not occurred in our experience with ESL students. Invariably, they have greeted poetry with remarkable enthusiasm; in an ESL class, there is no need to open with an apology.

Poetry is a particularly effective tool for practicing a particular grammatical structure because its very nature demands that it be spoken, repeated, wrestled with, and considered. With each repetition and consideration, the structure becomes more deeply internalized. Therefore,

[4] See Shaw.

poetry is an excellent resource for structured practice of grammar and an appropriate basis for review. If a poem that exemplifies a particular structure is also a good poem, it engages the eye, ear, and tongue simultaneously while also stimulating and moving us; this polymorphic effect makes poetry easier to memorize than other things for many students. A poem's capacity to comfort us in quiet, private moments also accounts for its popularity, and thus its effectiveness as a resource. How many other teaching aids can claim to engage students so deeply?

These benefits notwithstanding, the real problem with using poetry, of course, is that it is often difficult for non-native speakers to understand and seldom provides the structural repetition required of a good structure-practice resource. On the other hand, its benefits far outweigh the drawbacks, as long as one can rely on other resources for the structured phase of a grammar lesson. As for its incomprehensibility, Povey has characterized the three main "humps" or barriers to using English literature (including poetry) with foreign students as linguistic, cultural, and intellectual.[5] Linguistic problems include such things as syntax and lexicon, which are certainly of a higher level of difficulty in poetry than prose. Cultural barriers include imagery, tone, and allusion. Finally, Povey mentions the intellectual maturity and sophistication necessary to appreciate, relate to, and generally comprehend a poem's subject matter. Many experienced teachers are aware of these obstacles intuitively and have dismissed the possibility of using serious poetry in the ESL classroom because they seem insurmountable. However, in our experience, such potential problems can, in fact, be minimized, and poetry can provide an exceedingly rich and enjoyable context for ESL students.

Selection Guidelines

To begin, select a poem that displays the grammatical structure you would like to practice or review, or the structures you would like to contrast. We suggest beginning with 20th-Century poets: W. H. Auden, Robert Frost, Stanley Kunitz, Delmore Schwartz, W. D. Snodgrass, Theodore Roethke, Gary Snyder, Richard Wilbur, and Robert Lowell, to mention only a few. All provide excellent and

[5] Personal communication.

appropriate works to begin with. You might go to the library and thumb through their works or browse through an anthology for a poem that contains the structures of interest. Also, texts such as those by Laurence Perrine (1977) and Ciardi and Williams (1975) provide a variety of poems by various authors and extensive commentary for the teacher who is reluctant to present a poem to a class without having read a discussion of it first. Works with unusual syntax and lexicon should be avoided, although asking students to paraphrase a poem in standard syntax can be a very useful structured exercise. Try to pick a poem that will be relevant and meaningful to your students.

If the topic or point of view is interesting or controversial, the poem can provide a topic for discussion or written rebuttal, or become the basis for values clarification or cultural enlightenment through comparison or example. For example, Auden's "The More Loving One" naturally leads to an excellent discussion topic: Would you rather love or be loved and why? What kind of experiences might lead someone to make a statement such as, "If equal affection cannot be/ Let the more loving one be me." What might encourage the opposite point of view? Our students have found the topic fascinating, and they also enjoy the intellectual "workout" a difficult poem affords. In addition to exemplifying participials, hypothetical conditionals, and generic conditionals, this poem can also lead to a discussion of register and the circumstances under which expressions such as *go to hell* and *don't give a damn* might be heard and used. It also demonstrates the rather interesting effects of unexpected register shifts.

Teaching Procedures

Once the poem has been selected, the teacher might introduce it to the class by enthusiastically saying something like, "Listen to this! This is American poetry. Listen for the music that the poet manages to create with words." The poem can then be read aloud to students several times. Some may choose to close their eyes. You will probably be surprised at how much they enjoy listening as you read. After the poem has been read at least twice, elicit a discussion of students' initial response. Then distribute the poem to students and read it again aloud while they follow along.

The second step is to point out that poetry often has rather unusual syntax. Students can then paraphrase the poem in normal syntax. For example, the first line of Robert Frost's "Stopping by Woods on a Snowy Evening" would be paraphrased as, "I think I know whose woods these are." The poem should be paraphrased, sentence by sentence, with unknown words being defined as the class works through the poem. The paraphrased version is written on the board as it is elicited so students understand at least the surface meaning of the poem by the time they have worked through it. In this way, the first Povey "hump" of linguistic difficulty is minimized. After the poem has been paraphrased, read it again to weld it back together. Obviously, all of these readings reinforce the grammatical structure under consideration.

The third step is to ask questions about content. In the case of the Frost poem, one might pose questions such as, "Why won't the owner of the wood see the individual stopping?" "Why does he stop?" "Why does the horse shake its harness bells?" "What sounds does the individual hear?" "What time of year and time of day is it?" "Does the individual stay as long as he wants to?" "Why or why not?" These questions and any additional information the teacher can provide help lower the second Povey "hump" of cultural difficulty. For example, the teacher can share his experience with the subject matter—in this case, with snow and the woods— and perhaps even provide some pictures. Such touches are particularly helpful if your class is located in an area where snow is scarce or nonexistent. The important thing is to motivate students to report their experiences. The goal is to make the cultural content of the poem as real and vivid to students as possible. The sounds, sights, smells, and associations this poem evokes in a native speaker of English may elude a Middle Eastern student who is unfamiliar with snow, evergreens, and the "darkest evening of the year." Words, pictures, and shared experiences can bridge the gap. It's important not to skimp on this step. After the class has thoroughly discussed the surface content of the poem, read it once again and ask students to close their eyes and try to visualize whatever images the poem suggests to them.

The fourth step is to review the plot of the poem again and ask students if the poem might refer to something besides a frustrated desire to watch snow fall in the woods. Responses may not pour forth immediately, but if asked a sufficient number of artful questions, students

will eventually begin to discover deeper meaning. Avoid telling students
what the poem "means." If it is to become special to them, each must
discover his or her own meaning. Once students have begun to grasp
some of the depth of the poem, assist them in relating that meaning
to their own lives and experiences. Often it is difficult to relate an
abstract concept to experience, and the pump might require a little
priming. Once students get the idea, their contributions come quickly in excited bursts. This procedure helps to minimize the intellectual
challenge a poem poses, Povey's third "hump."

These four steps make a poem less complex and turn it into
a useful context for the practice of grammar. During the discussions,
no error correction should take place. The teacher's aim throughout
should be to provide support for the students in their efforts to understand the poem and make it relevant to their lives. Once they have
understood it and perceived its relevance, they will have no objection
to practicing the poem or even memorizing it, for it will have become
special to them.

For the next several days, the grammar lesson can be reinforc-
ed with a few minutes' practice. Students can read the poem line by
line after the teacher or read it aloud to each other in pairs. They can
even practice it with a partner in an attempt to memorize it. If due
care has been given to the process outlined above, and if the poem was
an appropriate choice to begin with, students will enjoy the challenge.
If your students do memorize the poems, allow them to demonstrate
their competence by reciting the poem to you or the class.

Example Poems

One of the poems mentioned above that we have used in our ESL classes
follows. This Auden poem can be used for conditionals, participials,
or logical connectors:

The More Loving One

> Looking up at the stars, I know quite well
> That, for all they care, I can go to hell,
> But on earth indifference is the least
> We have to dread from man or beast.

How should we like it were stars to burn
With a passion for us we could not return?
If equal affection cannot be,
Let the more loving one be me.

Admirer as I think I am
Of stars that do not give a damn,
I cannot, now I see them, say
I missed one terribly all day.

Were all stars to disappear or die,
I should learn to look at an empty sky
And feel its total dark sublime,
Though this might take me a little time.

W. H. Auden

The next poem has an interesting integration of tenses and is excellent
for a review of what structure to use when referring to different times
in English:

The Road Not Taken

Two roads diverged in a yellow wood,
And sorry I could not travel both
And be one traveler, long I stood
And looked down one as far as I could
To where it bent in the undergrowth;

Then took the other, as just as fair,
And having perhaps the better claim,
Because it was grassy and wanted wear;
Though as for that the passing there
Had worn them really about the same,

And both that morning equally lay
In leaves no step had trodden black.

Oh, I kept the first for another day!
Yet, knowing how way leads on to way,
I doubted if I should ever come back.

I shall be telling this with a sigh
Somewhere ages and ages hence:
Two diverged in a wood, and I—
I took the one less traveled by,
And that has made all the difference.

Robert Frost

Stanley Kunitz's "Benediction" provides practice of the subjunctive, as well as some lovely wishes for a very close friend.

Benediction

God banish from your house
The fly, the roach, the mouse

That riots in the walls
Until the plaster falls;

Admonish from your door
The hypocrite and liar;

No shy, soft, tigrish fear
Permit upon your stair,

Nor agents of your doubt.
God drive them whistling out.

Let nothing touched with evil,
Let nothing that can shrivel

Heart's tenderest frond, intrude
Upon your still, deep blood.

Against the drip of night
God keep all windows tight,

Protect your mirrors from
Surprise, delirium,

Admit no trailing wind
Into your shuttered mind

To plume the lake of sleep
With dreams. If you must weep

God give you tears, but leave
Your secrecy to grieve,

And islands for your pride,
And love to nest in your side.

Stanley Kunitz

Hulquist suggests Eleanor Farjeon's "The Night Will Never Stay" to practice *will* + uninflected verb to signal "inevitability" rather than future time.

The Night Will Never Stay

The night will never stay,
The night will still go by,
Though with a million stars
You pin it to the sky;

Though you bind it with the blowing wind
And buckle it with the moon,
The night will slip away
Like sorrow or a tune.

Eleanor Farjeon

The following poem by Edna St. Vincent Millay is particularly well suited to practicing the present perfect:

What Lips My Lips Have Kissed

What lips my lips have kissed, and where, and why,
I have forgotten, and what arms have lain
Under my head till morning; but the rain
Is full of ghosts tonight, that tap and sigh
Upon the glass and listen for reply,
And in my heart there stirs a quiet pain
For unremembered lads that not again
Will turn to me at midnight with a cry.
Thus in the winter stands the lonely tree,
Nor knows what birds have vanished one by one,
Yet knows its boughs more silent than before:
I cannot say what loves have come and gone,
I only know that summer sang in me
A little while, that in me sings no more.

Edna St. Vincent Millay

CONCLUSION

Of course, you do not have to restrict your choices to examples of famous poetry. Some teachers write their own limericks to illustrate grammatical structures, while some prefer to use a verse or two from Ogden Nash. (We know of one teacher who even writes her own songs for use in the classroom.) Not all students like songs and poems, but they might be more receptive to this more "creative" type of practice than you think, provided they know why they are doing it and what they should be learning. The important thing to keep in mind is that songs and verse provide rich, engaging contexts that, because of their appeal, make it easier to internalize structures.

· ACTIVITIES ·

Discussion Questions

1. Have you ever used songs to teach or learn a language? How did students respond? Why might some students object to the use of songs in a language class? How would you, as a teacher, respond to such objections?

2. Are there any poems or songs which you feel would be particularly useful in an ESL grammar lesson? Share them with your colleagues and explain why you feel they would be helpful to students.

Suggested Activities

1. Go to a library and check out an anthology of English poetry. Thumb through it and see if you can find at least two poems to teach two particular structures. Share them with your colleagues.

2. Find two songs which you could use to teach two particular structures in English. Share them with your colleagues.

3. Find a language teacher who uses songs or verse in his or her classroom. Arrange to observe class on a day when he or she is going to use songs or verse and then answer the following questions: How did students react? Did they participate enthusiastically? What techniques did you observe that you would like to adapt/adopt in your own classroom? What would you not adopt and why?

·CHAPTER TEN·
Techniques and Resources Integrated

GAMES AND PROBLEM-SOLVING ACTIVITIES

When ESL students are engaged in games or problem-solving activities, their use of language is task-oriented and has a purpose beyond the production of correct speech. This makes these activities ideal for communicative practice of grammar if, in fact, the activities can be structured to focus learners' attention on a few specific forms before the communicative practice. When this is successfully achieved, problems and games help reinforce a form-discourse match, since the form(s) targeted for attention occur naturally within the larger discourse context created by the game or the problem.

Following Maley (1981), we are grouping games and problem-solving activities together in this chapter because we believe they are similar in many respects. As Johnson (1973) indicates, games have a goal, are organized according to rules, and are meant to be enjoyable. Problem-solving activities also have a goal (i.e., the solution of the problem), and although they rarely have elaborate game-type rules, the problems themselves may be structured so as to require unique and creative solutions.

When using games or problem-solving activities, the ESL teacher must be sure that students are familiar with the words and structures needed to carry out the task. Quick drills or exercises should usually be done before students play the game or solve the problem. This will encourage them to practice the appropriate forms rather than the pidgin-like forms that may result when second-language learners are forced to engage in a communicative task before they have sufficient command of the words and structures needed to accomplish it.

Because games and problem-solving activities are open-ended

and complex, they are best suited to students beyond the beginning level who have mastered sufficient vocabulary and grammar to be able to carry them out.

GAMES

While most ESL teachers agree that games are excellent learning activities for children, some believe that adult students are not receptive because they require something more than "fun and games" from their ESL classes. From our experience, well-planned games can teach and reinforce grammar points very successfully if the activities are geared to students' proficiency, age, and experience and are not presented condescendingly.

"The Treasure Hunt" is the first game we suggest beause it can be used successfully even with high-beginning or low-intermediate students. For this game—which elicits communicative practice of imperatives and potentially all types of questions (*yes/no*, *wh-*, alternative)—the teacher first divides the class into groups of three. (In a large class students could form groups of four or five.) Each group is given a small picture of a pot of gold—or some other appropriate "treasure"—with the group's number written on it in large script. The group is also given a thumb tack or a strip of masking tape and asked to select one of its members for a very important task.

The group members who have been selected for the important task step outside the room with the teacher and are told to hide the pot of gold in some secluded but accessible location at least fifty paces away from the classroom door. At this stage they should be instructed only to find a very good hiding place for the treasure as quickly as possible and return to the classroom.

Once all class members in charge of hiding the treasure have returned, they are told to rejoin their groups but to say nothing until further instructed. They are then told to give careful oral instructions to the other group members as to exactly where they must go to find their group's treasure. These instructions should be verbal only. No maps, gestures, or written notes are allowed. The other group members may ask as many questions as they wish. The one who hides the treasure must tell the others how to get from the classroom to the hiding place, not simply where it is.

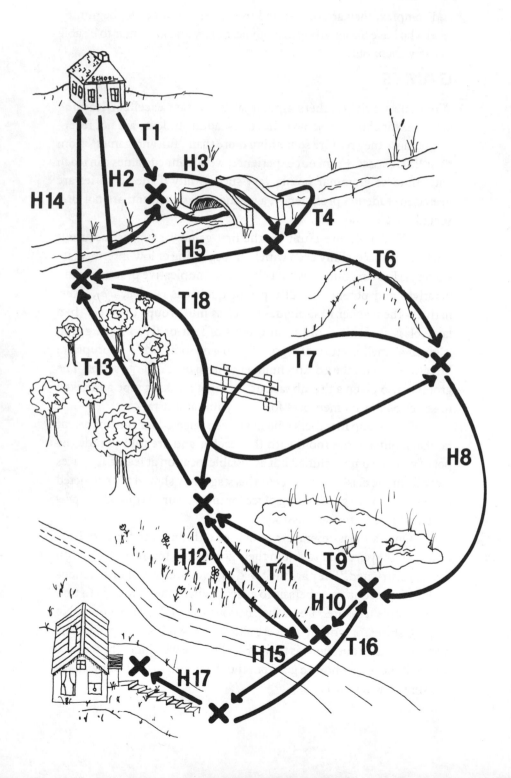

The teacher should point out that English speakers typically use imperatives and a variety of question types to give instructions and gather information in a situation. Appropriate models should be provided:

S1: Go out the door and walk down the hallway.

S2: Should we turn left or right when we leave?

S1: Left, but then go right at the first corridor.

S3: How far down the corridor should we go?

When the group members have received their instructions, they go out of the room and attempt to recover their treasure. If they become confused, they can return to the classroom for clarification or repetition. The first pair to find its assigned treasure and return to the classroom wins. The teacher can time all the groups and record how long it takes for each group to return. After a specified amount of time (about ten to fifteen minutes), all participants must return to the room, even if they haven't found their treasure. Time permitting, those groups that do not find their gold can locate the treasure and figure out why they did not find it. They should be able to explain what went wrong in their communications.

The title of our second game is "The Way Home," a board game for structured practice and reinforcement of prepositions of direction and the future with *going to*. Each group of four students needs a game board (reproduced on a piece of posterboard), a set of answer cards to consult as necessary, one coin to toss, and four identical bottle caps, each marked with a different number.

The board consists of the 18 paths that each player follows to get from school to home with ten locations or obstacles along the way.

The answer cards for the game look like this:

front of cards	*back of cards*
1.	I'm going to go/walk/run to the bridge.
2.	I'm going to swim/wade to the bridge.

front of cards   *back of cards*

3.	I'm going to go/walk/run over the bridge.
4.	I'm going to swim/wade/crawl under the bridge.
5.	I'm going to go/walk/run back to the riverbank.
6.	I'm going to climb/go/walk over the hill.
7.	I'm going to jump/climb/go over the fence.
8.	I'm going to go/run/walk around the pond.
9.	I'm going to walk/run/go to the meadow.
10.	I'm going to walk/run/go to the road.
11.	I'm going to walk/run/go to the meadow.
12.	I'm going to walk/run/go to the road.
13.	I'm going to walk/run/go through the forest.

front of cards	*back of cards*
14.	I'm going to go/walk back to school.
15.	I'm going to go/walk across the road.
16.	I'm going to go/walk/run back to the pond.
17.	I'm going to go/walk/climb up the stairs.
18.	I'm going to go/walk/run around the fence.

The four players draw the upside-down bottle caps (numbers on the top side) to see who will go first, second, etc. They all start at school. Each player in turn tosses the coin to determine his path (H for heads or T for tails). To continue, he must then announce the move he will make in the future using *going to* and the correct preposition. If the toss sends him back to an earlier obstacle, he must move back whether he can produce the correct utterance or not.

For example, a player begins at school and tosses heads. He must then say, "I'm going to go/walk/run to the bridge" before he can carry out this forward movement with his bottle cap. If he cannot orally express the move, or if he makes a language error his partners can detect, he loses a turn but may consult the set of eighteen answer cards that have the path numbers on one side and some of the most frequent responses on the other to see what is required so his next attempt can be successful. If after going over or under the bridge the same player next tosses heads, he must follow the arrow and return to the river-bank whether he can say what he is going to do or not. If he cannot say it, he should consult the answer card, produce the correct utterance, and then move his bottle cap back. Forward movement is the reward for producing a correct utterance; losing a turn is the penalty for not doing so, except in the case of backward movement, which is mandatory. (This is so a clever student does not figure out that purposely producing an incorrect response will prevent his having to move backwards.)

The numbered sides of the cards should always be face up. The answer cards or the teacher may also be consulted if one player wishes to challenge what another player has said. If a challenge is successful (i.e., the player trying to move gives the wrong information or makes an error), the player trying to move loses a turn and the challenger has an extra toss of the coin on his next turn. If the challenge is unsuccessful (i.e., the player trying to move makes an acceptable response), the player makes normal progress and the challenger loses a turn. There are sometimes disputes during such challenges that the teacher has to mediate and resolve.

The first player in each group to "get home" wins the game. If the class is at a beginning level, the diagrams and verbal descriptions on the answer cards should be practiced and reviewed carefully before the groups start to play the game. If the class is intermediate or advanced, it might be better to let them discover and learn a few unfamiliar items from the cards as they play.

The third and last game we will suggest is "Bid and Swap," a card game designed to provide communicative practice of the use of mass and count nouns, where the mass noun represents the class noun and the corresponding count nouns represent specific members of the class. This game encourages practice of *some (mass noun)* , *a piece of (mass noun)* , as well as requests with *will* that are typical of trading or bartering contexts.

Each group of three to five players is given a set of twenty-five cards. Five of these pictures should represent class nouns such as furniture, clothing, fruit, luggage, and fish. The remaining twenty pictures should represent four specific members of each of these five classes (e.g., a chair, a table, a desk, and a sofa—for furniture).

As soon as everyone is familiar with the vocabulary and aware of which cards represent class nouns and which specific nouns (this can be practiced in the groups), all the picture cards are shuffled and placed face down on the group's table or desk.

There are two parts to this game. First, each member of the group (the turn sequence may be established by a toss of the dice) asks

for a class of pictures by saying, "I need/want *some* *(mass noun)* ."
After each bid, the top card of the stack is turned face up. If the bidder's choice appears as the card for the class noun (e.g., fruit) or the card for a member of the class (e.g., banana), the bidder keeps that card, hides it from the others, and then gets an extra turn. If the bidder's choice does not appear, the card is placed face down at the bottom of the stack. This continues until all the cards are in the possession of the players. (The stack of cards will probably have to be replayed several times before this happens.) Second, once all the picture cards have been acquired, the players take turns trying to make trades in order to complete one set of five pictures as quickly as possible. (Again, a roll of the dice can be used to determine this sequence.) The barter offered can be a general item for a general item, a general item for a specific item, a specific item for a general item, or a specific item for a specific item. For example:

> S1: Ali, will you trade a piece of furniture for a piece of fruit (a banana)?

Ali responds "yes" or "no" and makes his own bid:

> S2: Marco, will you trade a shark for a piece of clothing (a dress)?

The player being addressed by the trader can say either "yes" and make the trade or "no." The latter, of course, is ambiguous and can mean either "I don't have it" or "I don't want to trade." In either case, the next player can then propose a trade, continuing in this manner until there is a winner. The winner is the first player to complete a set of five cards—the class noun plus all four member nouns (e.g., *furniture/chair*, *table*, *desk*, *sofa*). A trade may result in a tie with two winners.

PROBLEM-SOLVING ACTIVITIES

Problem-solving activities rank high in most accounts of communicative language teaching. Brumfit (1984), for example, reports on some promising experimental work in South Indian schools where the *Procedural Syllabus* has been implemented. This is an approach to second-language teaching developed by Prabhu based almost exclusively on the use of highly challenging problem-solving activities. Similarly, Widdowson (1986) has encouraged extensive use of problems, such as the following for communicative language teaching:

There was a farmer who had to get himself, his dog, his chicken, and a bag of grain across the river. Unfortunately, his boat was so small [that] the farmer could carry only the dog, the chicken, or the grain during one crossing. Also, he could not leave the dog with the chicken because he would eat her, and he could not leave the chicken with the grain because she would eat it. What did the farmer do to get himself and everything else across the river safely?

Although such problems provide an excellent opportunity for language practice, it is hard to get students to focus systematically on one or two structures while solving them. The problem above could elicit conditional sentences, or sequential logical connectors, or causal logical connectors, or a host of other structures. Thus, as a resource for teaching grammar, the problem is too diffuse unless the teacher finds a way to provide a structural focus. Communicative practice involving problem-solving activities should naturally elicit and focus on a smaller range of structures, and it is this type of narrowly focused problem-solving activity that we will concentrate on in this chapter.

The first activity is a fairly simple one called "Where Were You Born?" In classes in which students come from a wide variety of places, this exercise can provide communicative practice of this common passive-voice question and corresponding answers, which occur in the past tense in English rather than the present tense, as is the case in many other languages.

At the end of one class session, the teacher distributes three-by-five index cards and asks each student to write down his name and the name of the town or nearest large city where he was born. During the next class session, students form groups of four or five, and each group receives one sheet that contains a list of the names of all class members and another that contains a list of all the places where the class members were born. Each group should select a secretary to keep track of the information.

The teacher should allow about ten minutes for the groups to record the birthplace next to the name of every student on the list. Students should guess if they are not sure. Before the exercise, the teacher should provide a model group conversation such as the following:

S1: I was born in Lima.

S2: I'll put that down. Where were you born?

S3: I was born near Havana. Where was Li born? Shanghai or Taipei?

S4: I don't know. I know José was born in Monterrey.

S5: Li was born in Taipei.

The group with the largest number of correct matches wins.

If most students were born in the same town, the teacher can use their dates of birth instead of the places of birth. Both pieces of information require use of the past tense of *to be born*.

Our second suggestion for a problem-solving activity is called "Lost on a Desert Island." It involves a problem that students should be assigned individually for homework so they can select choices for the seven most important items in preparation for resolving the following problem in class:

You are one of four surviving crew members of a small ship that sank off the coast of a large desert island. You and your companions must now walk some 100 miles to the other side of the island where other ships are much more likely to pass. You will then be able to signal one of these ships to pick you up. Much of the equipment on board sank with your ship. Because survival depends on your reaching the other side of the island where you can signal passing ships, you must choose the seven most critical items for the 100-mile trip, since you are all weak and cannot carry everything.

Listed below are the fourteen items that the four of you were able to rescue. Your task is to select the seven most important ones with the goal of eventual rescue. You must defend each choice with a good reason.

Items

a box of matches	4 gallons of water
50 feet of nylon rope	a first-aid kit
a portable stove	two signal flares
a flashlight with batteries	two .45 caliber pistols
a magnetic compass	a case of powdered milk
a life raft	a solar-powered FM
a world map	receiver-transmitter
some food concentrate	

Answer any questions regarding vocabulary, grammar, or the task in general when the problem is first presented. The grammatical objectives for this lesson are:

1. communicative practice of article usage with reference to the count and mass nouns on the list of objects
2. the use of the comparative and/or superlative degree(s) in deciding which items are among the seven most important ones

There will also be some use of logical connectors of reason or purpose, such as *because* (*in order to*), when students try to convince each other in case of conflicting priorities. Before the class divides into groups to discuss the problem, the teacher should model one possible argument in order to focus practice appropriately. For example:

"The life raft is the least important item since they have to walk across the island, not travel by water."

The teacher could also ask students to offer a few more arguments before the group work begins:

"The water is more important than the milk because . . ."

"We'll need the matches to light the flares."

Each group is given fifteen minutes to arrive at a concensus. Individual students will probably have made slightly different selections on their own, so it will be up to them to debate and decide among themselves which seven items are, in fact, the most important ones.

When the fifteen minutes have elapsed, each group should write its list of the seven most important items on the board so results can be compared across groups. Any discrepancies should be noted and, if possible, resolved by the class as a whole.

Our third and final problem, "Decisions, Decisions," is adapted from Rosensweig (1974), who suggests a personal student-centered dilemma in the values clarification genre. We recommend a format such as the following, which has two phases.

On the first day, the teacher presents the problem below to the students, along with a list of possible responses:

A good friend of yours is a foreign student in the United States and is midway through his Ph.D. in physics. He has only two more years remaining on his scholarship from the Ford Foundation. Things were progressing smoothly, but now he has received a letter from home saying his mother is seriously ill. His family wants him to return home until his mother recovers, an indefinite period of time. However, if he decides to go home, he will leave behind a girlfriend he is thinking of marrying. It is possible that should he go home, he won't see her again. Professionally, he knows his country needs physicists for its development, so he feels pressured to complete his studies. Being a physicist is also an important career goal for him. If he goes home, he risks losing his scholarship, since it is not given to students who interrupt their education.

Your friend has just written you a long letter explaining his problem in great detail. What would you advise him to do? Listed below are nine possible suggestions you can make to your friend. Place the number *1* by the best suggestion, *2* by the second best suggestion, and so on. Do this first at home tonight; and then in your groups during the next class, you will have twenty minutes to reach a consensus on your rankings.

Rankings

Individual	Groups	
		Go back to your country to help your family.
		Get married and go back home with your new spouse.
		Get drunk and forget about it for a couple of days.
		Write to your father to explain the situation and ask him what you should do.
		Plan a short trip home and then come back.
		Go back until your mother gets well, hoping to get your scholarship back.
		Get married in the United States and finish school.
		Write a letter to the Ford Foundation explaining the reasons for interrupting your education, and ask them for permission to leave and resume as soon as possible.
		Go back and try to finish your Ph.D. in a university in your country.

During phase two (the next day) before students compare their rank-ings, the teacher can point out that they should use expressions such as *I think (that)*. . ., *I suppose (that)*. . ., *I believe (that)*. . ., and other verbs of cognition that take *that* clauses. They also might use future conditionals to explore the various options the student has (e.g., *If he does that*, . . . *will happen*). They definitely will use modals and aux-iliaries of advice and persuasion such as *should, ought to*, and *had better* (e.g., *You had better go home. If you don't, you may never see your mother again*) and logical connectors such as *because* and *since* (e.g., *I think you should stay here and finish your studies because* . . .) when they de-fend the reasons for their rankings. There is, of course, no absolutely correct ranking for the choices provided in this activity. Preferences are usually a matter of personal or cultural bias.[1]

It has been our experience that students will use the structure they have been studying, particularly if the teacher requests that they do so. Therefore, this exercise could be used for communicative prac-tice of any of the above-mentioned structures, but students must be told the precise objective(s) of the exercise.

COMMENTARY

Most games and some problem-solving activities contain an element of competition. This is especially true if individual students, as opposed to teams or groups, are participating in an activity. Teachers may want to consider adapting such activities to make them non-competitive so there will be no "winners" or "losers." This is critical if the teacher senses that weaker students could get discouraged by always losing. If, however, the students are by nature highly competitive individuals, then such activities may be most effective if they are made as com-petitive as possible. The teacher will have to judge what is most ap-propriate for any given class. The personalities and preferences of students, not the personal philosophy of the teacher, should determine whether or not a competitive atmosphere is appropriate during games and problem-solving activities.

---

[1] Other sources where ESL teachers can find materials in values clarification or cultural problem-solving include Simon, *et al.* (1972), and Ford and Silverman (1981).

Once the task is understood and students—in pairs or groups, or as individuals—are ready to proceed, the teacher must carefully but unobtrusively monitor the class to check on comprehension and to see that the task is progressing. Any problems, questions, or conflicts that arise must be resolved while students are carrying out the task.

To promote communication and spontaneity during the game or problem, the teacher should correct as little as possible, intervening only when there is a factual misunderstanding or when communication breaks down. The teacher should note errors while the activity is in progress and then discuss the errors either with individuals or with the whole class after the activity is over. When several students are making the same error, we suggest that the teacher present a minigrammar lesson as soon after the activity as possible.

THE MINIGRAMMAR LESSON

An essential skill for any ESL professional is the ability to detect common systematic errors in the speech of students. Once detected, these errors should be remedied promptly if they are frequent enough during communicative practice to be distracting. This kind of correction can be done with a minigrammar lesson.

For example, imagine an intermediate-level ESL class doing the preceding "Decisions, Decisions" problem. Several students are saying sentences such as these, which the teacher notes for subsequent feedback and correction:

"You should to finish your studies because . . ."

"You must to go home because . . ."

"You should to write your father before you decide because . . ."

The error in these sentences is the use of the infinitive marker *to* after true modals—perhaps based on analogy with the maverick modal *ought to*, or with periphrastic forms of modals (e.g., *have to*, *be able to*, etc.), or with regular verbs that take infinitive complements (e.g., *try to*, *want to*, etc.).

The teacher can take a few minutes the next day to put these sentences on the board, explaining that they are the students' own sentences and asking the class what the problem is. Usually someone knows. If not, the teacher can rewrite, next to the sentences with the errors, the first four or five words of each sentence exactly as she would say them (i.e., without error). Rather than telling the class outright what the problem is, she can ask students to find the difference between their sentences and her sentences.

Once the errors have been detected and the rules elicited, the teacher can ask the class to generate two lists of verbs: (1) modals and modal-like forms that do not take *to* and (2) periphrastic modals and true verbs that require *to*. For example:

(1)	(2)
must	*have to*
should	*ought to*
will	*be going to*
could	*try to*
had better	*plan to*

Students can work in pairs and write short dialogs for a situation in which two college roommates are taking the same world history class. They are studying for the first exam and are trying to figure out what they should study and what the professor is going to ask on the test.

Task: What do the roommates say to each other?
        Write a short dialog. Use at least two verbs from each list.
S1: I'm sure he will ask about the Crusades.
S2: So what do we have to study?
S1: We should outline what happened from 1095 to 1270.
S2: Well, let's try to list the main events for a start.

The teacher can then check all the dialogs as they are being written and perhaps ask a few groups to read theirs aloud. The class should listen as the dialogs are read and correct them afterward if necessary.

To summarize, a minigrammar lesson consists of the following steps:

1. teacher presents relevant data (i.e., errors) to students
2. teacher, without lecturing, gets students to detect and correct the error(s)
3. teacher presents students with a warm-up exercise on the target structure(s) (e.g., has them generate a paradigm, make lists, do a cloze exercise, etc.)

4. teacher provides a contextualized, and if possible, a communicative task to practice the structure(s)

A skilled ESL teacher can, as needed, generate such a minilesson extemporaneously and teach it in about fifteen minutes. We feel that regular, well-timed use of such short lessons in response to systematic errors being made in class is one of the most effective feedback and correction strategies a teacher can provide her ESL students.

CONCLUSION

In this chapter we have suggested three games and three problem-solving activities that we feel can be used for extended communicative practice of grammar. Such activities encourage the learner to match grammar with discourse in the context of the game or the problem-solving activity. Since these activities are more complex than many of the exercises we have suggested earlier, students are expected to have a certain level of grammar and vocabulary proficiency before they take on such exercises. Finally, we presented the format for a minigrammar lesson, an important and essential remedial technique that ESL teachers should be able to provide in a timely fashion whenever needed.

·ACTIVITIES·

Discussion Questions

1. Could an entire course syllabus be organized around games and/or problem-solving activities? Explain why this would or would not be possible and/or desirable.

2. Is it important to put a time limit (and to enforce it) on all games and problems done in an ESL class? Why or why not?

3. Why is it desirable to allow some time for a postgame or postproblem discussion with the whole class whenever such activities are done in an ESL class?

4. Consider all the games and puzzles you have at home. Could any be adapted for use in an ESL class to teach grammar?

Suggested Activities

1. Adapt or develop a game that could be used to teach a structure not covered in this chapter. Try out the game with a small group of non-native English speakers and describe how it worked. How would you change or improve it?

2. If possible, look at one of the many books on using games to teach English to ESL/EFL students (e.g., Lee 1979, McCallum 1980, Rinvolucri 1985, Maley 1981, Wright, *et al.* 1984). Find a game with a grammar objective that you feel you could use with an EFL/ESL class. Share the game with others in your group.

3. Adapt the strategy for feedback and correction recommended in the minilesson portion of this chapter to an area of grammar you know causes problems for your students. What is the grammar area? What would you do at each step in the minilesson?

CHAPTER ELEVEN

Techniques and Resources Integrated

TEXT-BASED EXERCISES AND ACTIVITIES

During the past ten years great advances have taken place in the teaching of reading and composition in the ESL classroom. Work in reading theory done by Goodman (1970), Goodman and Goodman (1971), Smith (1982), and others, as well as work on the writing process done by Raimes (1983), Zamel (1983), and others have shown us that process is important. In other words, the steps, procedures, and strategies that we teach our students and encourage them to follow while reading or writing are ultimately as important as what they are able to read or write. In this chapter, we don't want to diminish or ignore what has been learned about the reading or the writing process with reference to ESL students. Rather, it is our intent to point out that grammar can play a small but important role in their reading comprehension (Schlesinger 1968) and a significant role in the perceived quality of their writing (McGirt 1984).

While most grammar instruction in the ESL classroom focuses on the sentence level, reading and writing activities engage the students at the "text" level (i.e., a semantically coherent piece of spoken or written discourse). Thus, if we want to teach grammar in a way that will facilitate transfer to our students' reading and writing, we must teach it at the text level, not just the sentence level. The activities suggested in this chapter, all of which match grammar with discourse, are some of the ways in which this can be accomplished. The primary technique is the comprehension and generation or manipulation of texts, and we start with the texts themselves as resources for creating a variety of activities.

Although beginning students can do some of the activities we

149

describe below, most of the exercises are more appropriate for inter-mediate and advanced ESL students who have the necessary control of basic sentence-level grammar to carry out a variety of reading and writing assignments.

The activities we stress in this chapter are especially relevant in the ESL composition classroom since in order for ESL students to use English grammar effectively and accurately in their writing, they need to develop an awareness of English structure that goes beyond sentence-level grammar drills.

TEXT REPLICATION

The most obvious and traditional, but nonetheless useful, text-based grammar exercises are dictation and dicto-comp. Both of these tech-niques can be presented visually or aurally, although the latter type of presentation is much more common, and both can require recall of a structure and integration of this structure into a meaningful text. Consider a passage such as the following:

> Many different kinds of students attend Northwestern Univer-sity. There are some who study, some who go to parties, some who play sports, and many who do all or most of these activities. There are students whose families pay their tuition and others who have been awarded scholarships. There are also a few who work and go to college at the same time. There are students who live on campus or who rent a room or apartment off campus. There are also some whose families live in the area, and many of them commute.

The teacher can use the passage as a dictation for structure practice of relative clauses with the relative pronouns *who* and *whose*. Secon-dary points might be existential *there* and use of quantifiers such as *some* or *many*, which are words that often occur with relative clauses in a paragraph such as this one, which deals with classification.

If used aurally, the teacher will read the passage once at normal speed, then a second time by reading one phrase at a time with pauses to allow for writing, and a third time by reading at normal speed but with pauses after each clause to allow for correction. If used visually, the passage is presented on the overhead projector and the class is instructed to read it all the way through. The passage is then visually presented phrase by phrase, but each phrase is removed from view as the class writes it down. Finally, the passage is shown once again in its entirety (students may only read, not write), after which students should be given a few minutes to make their final corrections. Teachers who have used both visual and aural dictation find that learners tend to make the same kinds of mistakes whether they listen and write or look and write.

There are a number of constructive ways in which dictations can be corrected. Some of the most elaborate suggestions are those given by Sawyer and Silver (1961), who recommend that each dictation be presented at three separate class meetings. First the dictation is given and the errors are underlined but not corrected; then students have their first effort with errors underlined in front of them as they take the dictation for the second time. Immediately after their second attempt is collected, a copy of the dictation is given to them to read. On the third administration, the teacher can reasonably expect students' work to be perfect, including spelling and mechanics.

The dicto-comp was first discussed in print by Wishon and Burks (1968). If the teacher presents the dicto-comp aurally (the usual way), the text is read about three times while the class listens. After each reading, the class may ask questions about words or phrases that confuse them, and they can discuss the gist of the passage, but they should not write anything other than key words or troublesome expressions. After the final reading, students try to reproduce the original as perfectly as possible. When they cannot remember the exact wording, they should use their best approximation.

The same thing can also be done visually. The teacher puts the passage on an overhead transparency and lets the class read it once. The teacher then removes the passage and lets students ask questions. After a second look at the passage, students are encouraged to discuss it after it has been removed. Following the third reading, the passage is removed and students try to reproduce it. Consider the following text:

When Ted was young he used to go out to the airport quite often to watch the planes taking off and landing. He saw all kinds of people coming and going. He listened to the speaker announ-

cing the flight numbers and destinations of the departing planes.
Whenever Ted heard her announce a flight leaving for Rome
or Athens, he imagined himself boarding the plane.

This can be used to practice or reinforce sensory perception verbs (e.g.,
watch, *see*, and *listen*) and the *-ing* complement pattern, which is one
of two patterns occurring after verbs of sensory perception.[1]

TEXT COMPLETION

There are two different kinds of text completion exercises: the cloze
passage and the gapped text. In a cloze passage, the blank spaces represent single words that have been deleted; in a gapped text, one or more
words are needed to fill each blank.

A cloze passage can be formed either by a random deletion process (i.e., every nth word deleted) or by a rational deletion process (i.e.,
specific items such as articles or prepositions deleted). The latter is
much better suited for focusing on specific points of grammar. Such
cloze exercises have long been used to teach grammar in context. In
the easiest type of cloze exercise, students simply have to choose between
two items [e.g., *a/an* or *the*, as in example (a) below] or two forms [e.g.,
gerund versus infinitive, as in example (b)].

a.   There was once ____(1)____ crow who stole ____(2)____
     wedge of cheese from ____(3)____ kitchen window. She flew
     off with ____(4)____ cheese to ____(5)____ nearby tree.
     ____(6)____ fox saw what ____(7)____ crow had done, and
     he walked over to ____(8)____ tree.
          "Oh, Mistress Crow, you have such lovely black feathers,
     such slender feet, such ____(9)____ beautiful yellow beak,
     and such fine black eyes! You must have ____(10)____ beautiful
     voice. Would you please sing for me?"
          ____(11)____ crow felt very proud. She opened her beak
     and sang CAW-CAW-CAW. Of course ____(12)____ cheese
     dropped down, ____(13)____ fox snatched it up and ate every
     bite.

[1] For further discussion of sensory verb complements, see Kirsner and Thompson
    (1976).

b.   Don't expect _____(1)_____ a Van Gogh painting in the same
      way you might enjoy a Renoir. Van Gogh will force you
      _____(2)_____ people, objects, and landscapes in a different
      way, a different light. He risked _____(3)_____ different and
      many who knew him thought he was insane. When he decided
      _____(4)_____, he did so to the exclusion of virtually
      everything else; this permitted him _____(5)_____ new
      dimensions in color, light, and texture. He particularly enjoyed
      _____(6)_____ in the south of France because of the sunlight
      and colors he experienced there.

      Note that (b) is not a "true" cloze exercise, since the choice of
an infinitive requires two words (i.e., *to* + verb). The gerund, however,
requires only one word, so use of this verbal is consistent with the definition of a true cloze exercise.

      Cloze exercises are more difficult if a large set of choices is in-
volved, such as in the following passage, where for each blank students
must fill in the best preposition of time or place:

      Thomas Mann, who won the Nobel Prize for Literature
      _____(1)_____ 1929, was born _____(2)_____ Luebeck, Germany,
      _____(3)_____ June 6, 1887. After finishing his studies _____(4)_____
      Luebeck, he went _____(5)_____ Munich, where his family had
      moved several years earlier. With the exception of the time he
      spent _____(6)_____ Italy _____(7)_____ 1896 _____(8)_____ 1898,
      Mann remained _____(9)_____ Munich _____(10)_____ 1933, at
      which time he exiled himself _____(11)_____ Switzerland because
      of his political differences with the Nazi regime.
            Mann stayed _____(12)_____ Switzerland _____(13)_____
      1938. _____(14)_____ that he came _____(15)_____ the United States
      and taught _____(16)_____ Princeton University _____(17)_____ two
      years.
            _____(18)_____ April, 1941, Mann took his family
      _____(19)_____ California, and they settled _____(20)_____ Pacific
      Palisades, a suburb of Los Angeles, _____(21)_____ 740 Amalfi
      Drive, a house that proved too small for the Manns and their six
      children. _____(22)_____ February, 1942, they moved _____(23)_____

a large house   _(24)_   1550 San Remo Drive, also
_(25)_   the Palisades. Here Mann lived   _(26)_   1942
_(27)_   1952, when he returned   _(28)_   Switzerland,
having become disenchanted with McCarthyism   _(29)_
the United States.

Mann died   _(30)_   August 12, 1955   _(31)_
Kilchberg, a small town   _(32)_   Zurich.

Such cloze exercises focus a learner's attention on many local aspects of grammar without ignoring the larger discourse; some typical teaching points for these exercises have been illustrated above.

Cloze exercises work best if students try to do them individually first and then compare their responses with a partner or with others in a small group. Serious differences should be reconciled with mediation from the teacher. It is important that each blank be numbered so discussion and correction can proceed without confusion.

Gapped text completion exercises typically are more difficult than cloze exercises, since students are required to supply more language. Again, enough text must be given to establish the context. Structurally related chunks of text can then be omitted to encourage practice of multiword structures in context. A gap exercise, like a cloze exercise, usually serves as focused practice or reinforcement rather than initial presentation. At the lower proficiency levels, a good gap exercise might be one that elicits *yes/no* questions in the form of a dialog. For example:

A: Hi, my name is José.
B: Glad to meet you. I'm Ivan.
A: _(1)_   ?
B: No, I study at USC.
A: _(2)_   ?
B: No, I study engineering.
A: _(3)_   ?
B: No, electrical engineering.
A: I haven't been doing too well. Why don't you ask a few questions?

Even if the teacher says nothing to the class, it is apparent that *yes/no* questions are being elicited. Students can do gap exercises as written reinforcement of the question forms they have been practicing. The teacher should get the class to review all the answers since there are usually several correct responses possible. This is another difference between cloze exercises, where frequently only one response is correct, and gap exercises. A more sophisticated gapped text might involve elicitation of the passive voice. For example:

> The local newspaper did a survey of which 1985 films the public liked best. The results were not surprising. *Prizzi's Honor* _____*(1)*_____ by 25 percent of those surveyed, while *Out of Africa* _____*(2)*_____ by 17 percent. *The Color Purple* _____*(3)*_____ by 15 percent and *The Trip to Bountiful* and *Witness* _____*(4)*_____ 12 percent each. No other film received more than 5 percent of the first-place votes.

Since gap exercises do not specify the number of words missing, they can be used to reinforce grammatical points that call for one or more words, such as tense. The following exercise (e.g., "Fill in each blank with the appropriate form of the verb indicated") is an example of a gapped text where one, two, or three words may be required in any given blank, depending on the context:

The audience in Dodger Stadium _____*(1)*_____ for almost 30 minutes
(wait)

when Michael Jackson finally _____*(2)*_____ onstage. Within seconds
(appear)

his band _____*(3)*_____ some music and his brothers
(play)

_____*(4)*_____ him. The crowd _____*(5)*_____ wildly. The much-awaited
(join)   *(cheer)*

"Victory Tour" _____*(6)*_____ .
(begin)

Even after Michael _____*(7)*_____ and _____*(8)*_____ for some
(sing)   *(dance)*

time, the crowd _____*(9)*_____ completely.
(not settle down)

Michael and his family ___(10)___ for two hours while colorful
                          (perform)
lazer light displays ___(11)___ and thousands of girls ___(12)___ .
                        (flash)   *(scream)*
It ___(13)___ a technically brilliant spectacle. Afterwards, most
      (be)
people who ___(14)___ there ___(15)___ it ___(16)___ the Jackson
              (be)   *(say)*   *(be)*
family's best performance ever.

TEXT MANIPULATION AND IMITATION

Text manipulation exercises were popular during the audio-lingual
heyday, when they were called "controlled composition." In spite of
this name, they have little to do with teaching composition; rather,
they are grammar exercises that provide students with practice in
making particular structure-discourse matches. Dykstra, *et al.* (1966)
and Paulston (1972) used exercises such as the following, in which
students are instructed to rewrite a past-tense narrative in the present
tense, to elicit contextualized practice of the third person singular
present inflection (and, coincidentally, adverbial expressions of
frequency):

> Sarah took her little sister Nancy to the park once a week. Nancy
> always went to the swings first. She wanted Sarah to push her,
> but Sarah soon grew tired of that. Sarah usually guided Nancy
> over to the slide, where Nancy climbed up and slid down several
> times while Sarah watched. Sometimes Nancy convinced Sarah
> to go on the see-saw with her for a while, but that never lasted
> very long.
>
> Nancy loved the park, and in her own way, Sarah did
> too. It was much better than being cooped up in their small
> apartment.

From a discourse perspective, this sort of text manipulation is
acceptable if students understand that the original text is a past habitual
narrative and that by putting it into the present tense they are produc-

ing a present habitual narrative.

In another example of this type of exercise, students rewrite a passage about someone named Lee. In the original, Lee is a girl. The task is then to rewrite the passage assuming that Lee is actually a boy. This involves changing all pronoun forms from *she* and *her* to *he*, *him*, and *his*, thus providing practice in distinguishing the gender of the various pronoun cases. This is particularly helpful at lower levels, especially with students whose native languages do not make a gender distinction for third person singular pronouns.

A more sophisticated text manipulation and imitation exercise occurs when the teacher provides students with a model passage drawn from literature, such as the following:

> After all these years I can picture that old time to myself now, just as it was then: the white town drowsing in the sunshine of a summer's morning; the streets empty or pretty nearly so; one or two clerks sitting in front of the Water Street stores, with their splint-bottomed chairs tilted back against the walls, chins on breasts, hats slouched over their faces, asleep. . . .
>
> Mark Twain, *Life on the Mississippi*

In their imitation of such a passage students must make a slight change of topic, such as writing about another place or another season. However, they should be instructed to retain the style and structure of the original passage as much as possible. The model above, for example, gives students practice in post-nominal adjectival phrases in context—especially *-ing* and *-ed* participles. The following passage was produced by one student who did this exercise:

> After all these months in America I can still picture my home town to myself now, just as it was when I left; the town sparkling under a blanket of white snow on a winter's afternoon; the streets full of Christmas shoppers. One Santa Claus sitting inside each large department store, with his huge chair placed carefully next to the Christmas tree, a white beard hanging from his chin, a red hat sitting on his head . . .

Another type of focused practice in structure-discourse matching that is often productive for intermediate and advanced ESL students is the use of text-based sentence-combining exercises, in which a scrambled sequence of simple sentences with a common structure or structures is presented, and the writer is asked to reorder the sentences and combine them into a coherent and cohesive text. The following illustration is adapted from a technique suggested in Slager (1973):

1. Now this old section is no longer a slum.
2. Many changes have been made.
3. New businesses have been started.
4. Education has not been neglected.
5. This section has been changed into an exciting place to live and work.
6. One old building had been converted into a theater.
7. A new college has recently been opened.
8. An old section of Portland has recently been restored.
9. New elementary and secondary schools have been built.
10. Cultural activities have been encouraged.

These sentences, which focus on the present perfect passive, can be reordered and combined into a paragraph such as the following:

> An old section of Portland has recently been restored. Many changes have been made. For example, new businesses have been started, and one old building has been converted into a theater because cultural activities have been encouraged. Education has not been neglected. New elementary and secondary schools have been built, and a new college has recently been opened. Now this old section of the city is no longer a slum; it has been changed into a new and exciting place to live and work.

Our final example of a text manipulation exercise involves using a transcribed conversation to elicit indirect speech. To save time the teacher could find a conversation in some published source, such as *The White House Transcripts*, or record and transcribe a conversation for class use. The conversation, which must be a self-contained text, should be about 150 words long, with several short exchanges. In the following example provided by Anne Ediger, the speakers are Myra and Bonnie, two UCLA students, and Cathy, their French instructor, who is a teaching assistant there in the French Department.

M: This is the first time I've ever had a class in a language where I haven't been afraid to speak the language. Usually I would never speak. But in your class I enjoy it.

B: Yeah. We have so much fun in this class!

M: I know. I'm just dreading next fall. I'll probably get some horrible person, who . . .

B: A biddy, some biddy!

C: Naw, we don't have any old biddies, except one, and she teaches grad courses.

M: Oh good. Well, I'll check 'em out and whoever I get, I'll come talk to you. I'll find out how their teaching is.

C: Okay.

B: You know, I was going to come down to you earlier in the course and say, "Look, if we give you a hard time, it's not because we don't like you. It's just that it's fun in your class."

C: No. I'd rather have it that way. I hated the first four weeks because I feel very uneasy when I just know that people don't want to talk to each other, or to me.

B: I thought the first four weeks were really interesting, I mean I was really fascinated by the language.

First, students can go over the authentic conversation with their instructor to be sure they understand it, and then the class can begin to convert the conversation (i.e., direct speech) into indirect speech, with the instructor writing on the board or the overhead projector. It is important to emphasize at this stage that not every single word needs to be reported; the setting and the speaker must be identified, and the facts and ideas expressed by the speakers must be conveyed. The instructor should point out that the selection of a reporting verb can help reflect the speaker's mood. For example:

> Bonnie and Myra are both students at UCLA. Cathy is their
> French instructor and a graduate student in the French Depart-
> ment. They are having a conversation over coffee after class.
> The end of the term is approaching.
>
> Myra *said* that it was the first time she had ever had a
> language class where she hadn't been afraid to speak the
> language. Usually she never spoke, but in this class she enjoyed
> speaking.
>
> Bonnie *exclaimed* that they all were having a lot of fun
> in the class . . .

At this point, the teacher can elicit some of the differences in tense,
person, and other expressions between the original conversation and
the written report. Then students can work in pairs or small groups
to complete the indirect report, asking questions as necessary. Each
pair or group should write out its version on a transparency so the class
can discuss and correct the different versions later and compare these
with the teacher's version. Finally, all the differences noted between
direct and indirect speech should be summarized, and students can
be given another dialog to convert into indirect speech as a homework
assignment.

For students who need to deal with academic topics rather than
general English, a transcribed interview with a specialist on an important topic could be used for this activity instead of a conversation.

TEXT ELICITATION

Because certain topics or tasks seem naturally to elicit certain structures, they should be more systematically exploited when teachers use
a text-based approach to grammar practice. For example, if the teacher
gives as a topic or title for a short essay, "What would you do if you
won a million dollars in the lottery?" then she should specify that
students use the hypothetical conditional (i.e., the subjunctive). This
provides both communicative and focused practice, since students
supply their own ideas while the teacher specifies the structure. A
student given this assignment might produce something like this:

If I won a million dollars in the lottery, first I would buy myself a car. I have always wanted a new car but have never been able to afford one. Second, I would go home at Christmastime to visit my parents because I have not seen them for almost two years. Then I would discuss with them what I should do with the rest of the money. They would give me good advice, which I would need, because I don't always spend my money wisely.

A small, task-based communicative project was suggested to us by Thom Hudson, who has successfully used a survey task with his ESL classes to practice the passive. First, his students conduct a survey using only native English speakers as their subjects. They gather some basic background information on each person interviewed (e.g., sex, nationality, occupation, area of residence) and then ask a fairly innocuous question (e.g., "What is your favorite TV program?") When they tabulate and write up their findings, the passive voice should occur with high frequency.

Models such as the following could be provided for the class:

TV Favorites: A Survey of 50 Americans
Fifty Americans living in Minneapolis were asked to identify their favorite TV programs during the week of May 12, 1986. "Dynasty" was mentioned most frequently (19 responses), then "Dallas" (9), and the third choice was "M.A.S.H." (6). No other program was mentioned more than three times.

"M.A.S.H." was selected by men more often than women (five men, one woman), whereas women preferred "Dallas" (eight women, one man). The votes for "Dynasty" were more equally divided (twelve women, seven men).

GRAMMATICALITY JUDGMENTS

There are certain times during an ESL lesson when the teacher may reasonably ask students to make grammaticality judgments; that is, the teacher can ask whether a sentence is grammatically correct and if not, why. Chaudron (1983) reminds us, however, that only as learners become more advanced do they become better at this type of activity; beginners are rather weak at making grammaticality judgments. Thus, the ESL teacher should probably emphasize explicit error correction activities with intermediate and advanced rather than beginning students. Chaudron also reminds us that intermediate students can best recognize and correct their own errors, while more advanced ESL students can effectively correct the errors of other learners in addition to correcting their own. Also, spending too much time on error correction with beginning students can be counterproductive, since beginners tend to correct erroneously (i.e., make correct segments incorrect).

Certainly the ability to recognize and locate an error precedes the ability to make an accurate correction. Thus, ESL teachers may elect to start raising learner awareness of correct and incorrect structures by asking students to find and label the correct and/or incorrect sentence(s) in a pair or set:

1. a. I enjoy to go to the movies.
   b. I enjoy going to the movies.
2. a. The girl speaks Italian is over there.
   b. The girl which speaks Italian is over there.
   c. The girl who speaks Italian is over there.

If students have difficulty with very analytical discussions of grammaticality and correctness, the teacher may want to begin to raise their awareness of form in this manner:

T: Class, most of you say (a) while I say (b). What's the difference?
   a. I have seen the movie yesterday.
   b. I saw the movie yesterday.

A few well-selected examples should precede some of the more demanding error location and correction activities suggested below. This type of activity can also be used in the presentation phase of a lesson to focus attention on a new structure, as a short review of previous lessons at the start of a class hour, or to correct an error after a communicative exercise. Remember, however, that only intermediate or advanced students should be asked to make grammaticality judgments.

One example of a more complex activity is for students to judge each sentence in a connected series as grammatical or ungrammatical.

	grammatical	ungrammatical
3. a. People who move to Los Angeles come for three reasons.		
b. First, city has a good climate.		
c. It is relatively warm and sunny all year long.		
d. Second, there is many jobs in Los Angeles since business and trade are centered there.		

Alternatively, the writing-error detection exercises often used by the Educational Testing Service and others testing language proficiency operate at a more local level and require students to identify which one of the three or four segments in each sentence of a text is ungrammatical:

4. a. <u>People who move to</u> <u>Los Angeles</u> <u>come to area</u>
                   a   b   c
    <u>for three reasons.</u>
              d

   b. <u>First,</u> <u>there has</u> <u>a good climate.</u>
         a   b   c

   c. <u>It is</u> <u>warm and sun</u> <u>all year long.</u>
        a   b   c

   d. <u>Second,</u> <u>there is many jobs</u> <u>because business and trade</u>
          a   b   c
    <u>are centered there.</u>
               d

Of course, once students become adept at locating errors, the next step is for them to be able to correct the errors. One of the easiest ways to start is for the teacher to present sentences with errors such as (1a) and (2a) and (2b) above and to elicit corrections from students. Beyond this, the teacher can present a coherent sequence of grammatical and ungrammatical sentences as in (3), so students must first decide whether the sentence is correct or incorrect and if incorrect, what the correct form should be. Likewise, a writing-error detection exercise such as the one in (4) can be expanded, so students not only locate but also correct the error in each sentence.

Two holistic approaches to error correction that are very promising but time-consuming are: (1) interview analysis for correction of oral production and (2) reformulation for correction of written production. In interview analysis (Wechsler 1987), the teacher-tutor records an extended conversation with the learner and transcribes exactly what the learner has said. The transcription then becomes the material used for error correction. The learner reads over the transcription and with the help of the teacher-tutor, when needed, corrects the mistakes with a colored pen and repeats the correct form aloud several times. In reformulation (Cohen 1983, 1985), the teacher-tutor takes a paragraph or essay written by the learner and rewrites it in his own words (i.e., overall organization and vocabulary items may get changed along with faulty grammar). The learner then compares his original with the teacher-tutor's reformulation to see, first of all, if the message has been preserved. Then he tries to understand why certain changes have been made. The discussion can, of course, be narrowed down to mechanics and spelling or to grammar if either of these is the area of greatest concern (e.g., because of error frequency or current pedagogical focus).

Since both interview analysis and reformulation are very time-consuming, they are more appropriate for private tutors rather than for classroom teachers, although teachers can adapt these techniques by getting their students to do some of the work. For example, a teacher can direct students to record a story about a memorable experience they had when they were young, transcribe the story exactly as it was told, and rewrite the story trying to avoid the errors made when the story was told. In such an adaptation, teachers supervise the work instead of trying to do it themselves. And by doing the work, students become that much more aware of their problems.

TEXT EDITING AND GRAMMAR CORRECTION AND FEEDBACK

It is always easier to correct someone else's written work than one's own. Using this generalization as a starting point, Witbeck (1976) proposes three peer correction strategies that are useful when the teacher wants students to focus on correcting specific grammatical errors during the editing process.

Witbeck suggests that paragraphs or short papers by students be used whenever possible and that papers be selected because they illustrate frequent error types, such as substitution of the present perfect for the simple past tense or overuse of the infinitive *to* + verb after modals. To ensure maximum focus, the teacher may even correct all other errors and ask students to do specific problem-solving correction activities, such as, "Find two verbs that need an *s* to show present tense," "Find four nouns that should take the definite article," etc. We recommend using explicit grammatical terminology with students, especially in classes where students already know it, although example errors and corrections or informal circumlocutions can also be used. All exercises presuppose that grammar points focused on in the activity have already been covered.

An alternative to Witbeck's use of student paragraphs or essays as sources of peer correction materials is to prepare a composite essay for group correction that illustrates similar errors from several students' written work. This avoids embarrassment by focusing on common problems. We have used this procedure, for example, to practice correction of tense and modal errors in conditional sentences with good results.

In large classes in which students write a lot, the teacher cannot correct everything. Instead, he can take an individualized approach by using a method called "the blue sheet." In this approach the teacher attaches a blue sheet to the paragraph or essay, lists two obvious structural errors made by the student, and refers the student to pages and exercises in the class grammar text pertinent to the two errors. Students do the assigned exercises when they get their blue sheets; the teacher then corrects them before the students rewrite their passages. We have found that such an item-by-item approach can yield good results over a period of time. The same approach could be used to identify and correct specific grammatical errors that the teacher has detected with some frequency in the students' speech.

Even in smaller classes, not every error needs to be corrected on every paper. In fact, such overkill tends to discourage students and thus impedes progress in the long run. Best results are achieved by focusing on one or two error types at a time, at least in the beginning.

An individualized checklist encourages students to focus when they edit and correct their own work. Its use is the next logical step in the grammar editing process and works best if, at first, short pieces of writing are used. When the teacher returns the first draft, grammar errors are underlined and major areas of difficulty are listed or checked off on the attached checklist. In this way, each student is aware of the errors he should correct as well as the location of the errors. Students should consult with the teacher or tutor if they do not understand what the errors are or how to correct them. Each student should keep these checklists and all the drafts of each writing assignment together in a notebook or folder. The teacher can then have individual conferences and, where necessary, refer students to additional exercises for those grammar areas in which errors are most persistent.

Students soon become adept at making such targeted corrections. As they progress, they should be asked to correct several structures already covered in class in passages in which the errors are only minimally indicated; for example, by underlining. Once the class (or the student) gets very good at editing by this means, neither the location nor the error type should be specified.

Some students respond better to a less judgmental correction procedure in which the teacher or tutor merely specifies rewordings for sentences or phrases that contain grammatical errors on an attached sheet. For example, consider this opening paragraph from an unedited ESL composition:

College Life

As a quarter begins, students are busy to choose the right classes for themselves. Right classes are which they can get a good grade from by the end of the quarter. The most concern issue of a college student is how he can do well on the examinations and receive a good transcript.

The attached sheet gives the following suggested rewordings:

> *the quarter*
> *busy choosing*
> *The right classes are those in which*
> *a good grade by the end of the quarter*
> *The greatest concern of a college student*
> *a transcript with good grades*

The student takes these suggestions into consideration when writing the second draft and asks for clarification if anything is confusing.

The best results are ultimately achieved if the teacher moves gradually from very focused correction procedures to less and less focused ones. Whichever error correction strategy is used, it is imperative that students incorporate the corrections and become aware of major grammatical problems. Over a period of time, these correction strategies, combined with systematic grammar instruction, have a positive effect on the accuracy of the writing produced by ESL students.

CONCLUSION

To ensure that students make a match between grammar and discourse we have argued the need for text-based grammar exercises and activities in all phases of grammar instruction: presentation, focused practice, communicative activities, and feedback and correction. Since reading and writing are text-based skills, grammar will transfer only if it is also practiced at the text level, and not simply at the sentence level.

Texts for such exercises can be found in anthologies, biographies, newspapers, magazines, textbooks, and students' own academic and personal writing.

Most of the writing activities we have suggested work best if the teacher—or a native English speaker—does them along with the class so that students can compare what they have written with the work of a native speaker.

We end this chapter with a caveat: grammar does not equal composition. Composition is a complex process that involves many phases for native and non-native alike: prewriting, composing, revising, editing, and rewriting.[2] As students edit their compositions and then rewrite them, grammar correction should be done as well. One of the biggest differences between ESL and native English students is that ESL students produce about seven to ten times more morphological and syntactic errors in their writing than native speakers.[3] Thus, by extension, ESL students need to do roughly seven to ten times more work on grammar editing and correcting than native speakers.

---

[2] See Raimes (1983) for further comments on this process.
[3] This was the ratio found in a controlled study by McGirt (1984).

·ACTIVITIES·

Discussion Questions

1. Do you agree or disagree with those who claim that grammar instruction has no effect on the quality of an ESL student's written work? Why?

2. Do you think the distinction the authors make between cloze and gap exercises is worth maintaining? Why or why not?

3. Witbeck feels that peer correction of ESL compositions is a good first step toward self-correction. Do you agree? Why or why not?

Suggested Activities

1. Find a text in a newspaper or magazine that makes frequent use of a particular structure. Then develop an activity that uses the text to practice the structure.

2. The "text elicitation" activities are the most communicative of all the writing exercises we suggested. Think of a good text elicitation activity that focuses on some structure other than the two illustrated in this chapter (i.e., hypothetical conditional and passive voice). Share it with your colleagues.

3. Below are the last two paragraphs of the composition on "College Life," written by the ESL student whose first paragraph was quoted above. Identify the errors and specify techniques and resources you would use to help the student correct them.

> Final exams period is the most intense and busy period for students. They have to finish their projects or papers before the finals. And they have to sure they know the class materials inside and out. So we see a lot of students staying up very late during this period. Black eyes and tired faces can be seen everywhere in the campus.
>
> As we see, the college pressures on students are so intense. For those who graduate from colleges, we know that they have gone through four years hardships and struggles.

·CONCLUSION·

In this volume we have argued that it is beneficial—if perhaps not absolutely necessary—for certain language learners with certain objectives in mind to study grammar. We have further suggested that teaching grammar entails helping learners perceive a relationship between grammatical structures and three other dimensions of language:

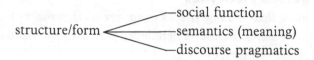

In our view, awareness of such relationships, or "matches," is critical to an understanding of grammar.

In making these matches, ESL teachers have various techniques and resources to draw on. For example, the technique of getting students to listen and respond to TPR-style commands (page 43) facilitates a match between form and meaning; the technique is best implemented by means of such resources as pictures, realia, and classroom objects. Many of the techniques and resources available for various matches are given throughout the book. We have focused only on the most useful. In addition, we have deliberately omitted such resources as language labs, media, video, and computers for two reasons: not all teachers have access to such technology, and an in-depth discussion of them is beyond the scope of this book.

Although our purpose has been to discuss the *teaching* of grammar, rather than facts about the language, we have introduced specific structures in two ways: We have varied the example structures throughout, with the result that most structures taught in beginning and intermediate courses are covered (some admittedly more thoroughly than others); and we have included a structure index so that the reader can easily locate all of our suggestions for specific structures, such as prepositions, articles, or phrasal verbs. In this way, we have tried to accommodate both the teacher who is looking for activities to enliven his classes and the one who puts grammar first.

We have emphasized the importance of teaching all aspects of grammar *in context*. Appropriate contextualization can only be achieved if a teacher finds or creates realistic social situations, language texts, and visual stimuli that are interesting and meaningful to students. Thus, contextualization is partly a matter of being faithful to the language, by finding appropriate examples, and partly a matter of being responsive to students, by taking their interests into account.

We have also discussed the four phases of teaching grammar: presentation, focused structure practice, communicative practice of structure(s), and feedback and correction. A single lesson might encompass one, two, three, or all four of these phases, depending on the amount of time available and the needs and level of the students. Specifically, some students who are relatively unfamiliar with a structure may require a careful introduction that includes examples in context and attention to form; others may have already mastered it to some extent but need practice. In still other cases, patterns of error may emerge over a period of time, say, in writing, and the teacher might then want to give these errors particular attention in correcting the students' work. This somewhat thorny question of correction is discussed in detail in Chapters Ten and Eleven.

Regardless of how well prepared a teacher is, how carefully she follows the plan we have outlined, and how skillful she is at error correction, she may still be unsuccessful if she cannot relate to students on a human level or understand their needs, interests, attitudes, and motivations. The ability to "read" students—to get beneath the surface and grasp the extent to which they are disposed to learn English—and to plan activities accordingly sometimes makes all the difference between a good class and a bad one.

This book contains many example activities, many of which specify that students should work in pairs or small groups. By this means, a teacher can ensure that a student participates optimally and takes partial responsibility for both her own learning and that of her classmates.

"Autonomous learning" and "peer-mediated instruction" have a long history in the language classroom (see Kelly 1976), but the whole notion of a learner-centered classroom was given a major boost with the emergence of the "Silent Way" as a popular approach to language learning in the 1970s (Gattegno, 1976).

Recent classroom research (e.g., Long 1977) has shown that students who spend a substantial portion of their time in small groups acquire more language than students whose teachers take a whole-class, lock-step approach. In short, controlling all student activity and having every student do the same thing at the same time is, generally speaking, less effective than breaking the class up and maximizing individual participation. On the other hand, some small-group configurations may be more effective than others, depending in part on the purpose of a class and the students' predispositions.[1]

Many teachers, perhaps out of a fear that they will lose control, hesitate to engage in small-group work. Such fears are not well founded, and perhaps have more to do with the subconscious assumptions about the role of a teacher than the value of such activities. Although a teacher may not be able to monitor all utterances all of the time, that does not mean that she has abdicated responsibility for what students learn or how they learn it. The teacher is not the only source of information about the language in the classroom; indeed, she may not even be the best one if her goal is to enable students to operate independently in a variety of domains. In short, there are powerful affective reasons for giving students room to struggle on their own, test themselves informally against each other, and develop a sense of community apart from the teacher's control. Her job, after planning her presentation, materials, and exercises, is to structure related activities that are consistent with the dynamics of the group. In this way, she ensures that all students have an opportunity to practice the language, whether the class is large or small, and develop the capacity to monitor their own output. The

[1] See Pica (1985) for a discussion of the relative effects of various groupings.

teacher is there to help them when needed.

Each ESL student is an individual who comes to class with special interests, needs, aptitudes, and attitudes to which a teacher must be responsive. Students in the same class often perform very differently, even if they all started at the same point and received the same instruction. We do not always know exactly why this happens. Some differences in achievement stem from differences in language-learning aptitude, general learning style, and the amount of time and attention students give the material. Student attitudes toward the teacher, her method, the target language, and the cultural values it embodies also play a role. In general, research (e.g., Oller, *et al.* 1977, Snow and Shapira 1985) suggests, somewhat predictably, that if a language learner likes the target language, his teacher, and other native speakers, then he is more likely to master the language. If, on the other hand, he doesn't like any or all of these, his learning is diminished. In such cases, a student's feelings about the dominant culture can sometimes feed his frustration with the cognitive demands of language learning and cause the whole process to break down. At that point, his failure to progress, his growing sense of inadequacy, and his generalized feelings of alienation can lead to antisocial behavior. The teacher may even become the target of his anger. As teachers, we overlook such factors at our peril. It is clear that they have a profound effect on how much and how quickly students learn.

In addition to attitudinal differences, students also have different motivations for learning a second language. Following Gardner and Lambert (1972), these are frequently broken down into two broad categories: integrative motivation and instrumental motivation. Some students want to learn English to become more like native speakers of the language; typically, these are students who have immigrated to an English-speaking country where they will live for the rest of their lives. They are for the most part happy to shed their primary cultural definition and acquire a new one. Their motivation is integrative. Others have a more narrow objective in mind, possibly a vocational or professional one, possibly one to be realized in the short term. For example, they may want specialized training in, say, business management or a medical specialization or word processing. For them, language study is only a means to an end, so their motivation is said to be instrumental. Regardless of which category a student falls into, his motivation may vary in intensity. In fact, some students may have no personal motivation for learning English. A teacher can only create conditions in which these differences—in both kind and degree—play themselves out.

In any case, all the factors we have discussed have an important influence on the language learning process. Obviously, some are beyond a teacher's control; ultimately, it is the student who must take charge of his own learning; the teacher is only a temporary assistant in the process. But it is useful to know what the factors are, partly because they help us understand differences in achievement among students and partly because they provide a principled basis for selection of materials and activities. Despite the teacher's limitations and the curious dynamics of a language classroom, she is never irrelevant. When all is said and done, as Hunter (1974) has observed, the single most important variable in determining student achievement is probably still the teacher: her knowledge of the subject matter, her ability to put it across, and her rapport with students.

We should add a final word about teacher-student relationships. We have sometimes observed well-intentioned teachers who were so sensitive to criticism and afraid that students would not like them that they were unable to curb unruly students, reluctant to correct errors, and incapable of politely refusing dinner invitations they did not want. In some cases, their reluctance to take charge, even of their social lives, left them feeling used and overwhelmed. Failure to establish a *modus operandi* with their students nearly drove them out of teaching.

Teachers who assume a highly professional attitude toward their students are the most effective. Such teachers prepare and execute lessons conscientiously and are not easily side-tracked by irrelevant comments or questions. They take a no-nonsense approach toward rudeness, class disruptions, and inappropriate behavior. By establishing limits, they command respect and create an atmosphere in which real learning can take place. By demonstrating their concern for the process, they create the conditions for real communication. They are able to be warm, sincere, and caring without compromising their dignity or professional standards.

We hope that you will be able to adopt and adapt many of the suggestions in this book. In the process, we hope that you will find them as exciting as we have. They have brought us many happy moments in the classroom, and if they turn out to be as pleasurable for your students as they have been for ours, then one of our major purposes in writing this book will have been achieved. But we don't want you to stop there. We hope we have provided you with a framework for the creation of classroom activities and exercises that belong, ultimately, to you and your students. As we have said, it is important for each of us to explore and develop techniques that are compatible with our own personalities and philosophies. This book is only a beginning. The rest is up to you. Whatever material and activities you produce we hope you will also share with colleagues at informal gatherings, workshops, and conferences. It would be a sweet bonus for us if this book contributed in some small way to the collective enterprise of teaching grammar in ways that are at once both pedagogically sound and sensitive to students' needs.

We wish you luck.

BIBLIOGRAPHY

Chapter One

Aitchison, J. 1985. "Predestinate Grooves: Is There a Preordained Language 'Program'?" *Language: Introductory Readings*, edited by V. Clark, P. Escholz, and A. Rosa. New York: St. Martin's Press, Inc.

Cronbach, L.J., and R.E. Snow. 1977. *Aptitudes and Instructional Method: A Handbook for Research in Interactions*. New York: Halstead Press.

Gleitman, L. 1986. "Biological Preprogramming for Language Learning?" *The Brain, Cognition, and Education*, edited by S. Friedman, K. Klivington, and W. Peterson. New York: Academic Press, Inc.

Hartnett, D.D. 1985. "Cognitive Style and Second Language Learning." *Beyond Basics*, edited by M. Celce-Murcia. Rowley, MA: Newbury House.

Hatch, E., *et al.* 1985. "What Case Studies Reveal About System Sequence and Variation in Second Language Acquisition." In *Beyond Basics*, edited by M. Celce-Murcia. Rowley, MA: Newbury House.

Higgs, T.V., and R. Clifford. 1982. "The Push Toward Communication." *Curriculum, Competence, and the Foreign Language Teacher*, edited by T.V. Higgs. Lincolnwood, IL: National Textbook Co.

Hyams, N. 1986. *Language Acquisition and the Theory of Parameters*. Dordrecht, The Netherlands: Kluwer Academic Publishers Group.

Landau, B., and L. Gleitman. 1985. *Language and Experience: Evidence from the Blind Child*. Cambridge, MA: Harvard University Press.

Lenneberg, E. H. 1967. *The Biological Foundations of Language*. New York: John Wiley & Sons, Inc.

Lightfoot, D., *et al.* 1983. *The Language Lottery*. Cambridge, MA: The MIT Press.

Long, M. 1986. "The Effective Instruction of Interlanguage Development." Lecture given at the University of California, Los Angeles, on February 14, 1986.

Madsen, H. 1983. *Techniques in Testing*. New York: Oxford University Press.

Newmeyer, F. 1983. *Grammatical Theory: Its Limits and Its Possibilities*. Chicago: University of Chicago Press.

Richards, J. 1985. *The Context of Language Teaching*. Cambridge, UK: Cambridge University Press.

Rutherford, W.S. 1987. *Second Language Grammars: Learning and Teaching*. New York: Longman.

Schumann, J. 1987. "Field Testing a Lexical Method for Language Learning." Paper presented at the Twenty-first Annual TESOL Convention, Miami, April 25, 1987.

Witkin, H. A., C. A. Moore, D. R. Goodenough, and P. W. Cox. 1977. "Field-Dependent and Field-Independent Cognitive Styles and Their Educational Implications." *Review of Educational Research* 47: 1–65.

Chapter Two

Anderson, R.W. 1978. "An Implicational Model for Second Language Research." *Language Learning* 28(2): 221–282.

Azar, B. 1981. *Understanding and Using English Grammar*. Englewood Cliffs, NJ: Prentice-Hall, Inc.

Bailey, N., C. Madden, and S. Krashen. 1974. "Is There a 'Natural Sequence' in Adult Second Language Learning?" *Language Learning* 24: 235–243.

Burt, M., and C. Kiparsky. 1974. "Global and Local Mistakes." *New Frontiers in Second Language Learning*. Rowley, MA: Newbury House.

Celce-Murcia, M., and D. Larsen-Freeman. 1983. *The Grammar Book*. Rowley, MA: Newbury House.

Chomsky, N. 1965. *Aspects of the Theory of Syntax*. Cambridge, MA: The MIT Press.

Cooper, R. (n.d.) *Language Planning and Social Change*. Cambridge University Press. In preparation.

Dulay, H., and M. Burt. 1974. "Natural Sequence in Child Second Language Acquisition." *Language Learning* 24(1): 37–54.

Frank, M. 1972. *Modern English: A Practical Reference Guide*. Englewood Cliffs, NJ: Prentice-Hall.

Larsen-Freeman, D. 1975. "The Acquisition of Grammatical Morphemes by Adult ESL Students." *TESOL Quarterly* 9: 409–419.

Larsen-Freeman, D. 1976. "An Explanation for the Morpheme Acquisition Order of Second Language Learners." *Language Learning* 26: 125–134.

Leech, G., and J. Svartvik. 1975. *A Communicative Grammar of English*. Essex, UK: Longman Group Ltd.

Master, P. 1986. "Measuring the Effect of Systematic Instruction in the English Article System." Manuscript; University of California, Los Angeles; Applied Linguistics Program.

Morrow, K., and K. Johnson, (eds.) 1981. "Principles of Communicative Methodology." *Communication in the Classroom*. New York and London: Longman.

Pienemann, M. 1984. "Psychological Constraints on the Teachability of Languages." *Studies in Second Language Acquisition* 6(2): 186–213.

Quirk, R., S. Greenbaum, G. Leech, and J. Svartvik. 1985. *A Comprehensive Grammar of the English Language*. London and New York: Longman.

Shintani, M. 1979. "The Frequency and Usage of the English Passive." Ph.D. dissertation; University of California, Los Angeles; Applied Linguistics Program.

Tomiyama, M. 1980. "Grammatical Errors and Communication Breakdown." *TESOL Quarterly* 14(2): 71–79.

Chapter Three

Asher, J. 1965. "The Strategy of the Total Physical Response: An Application to Learning Russian." *International Review of Applied Linguistics* 3: 291–300.

Asher, J., J. Kusudo, and R. de la Torre. 1974. "Learning a Second Language Through Commands: The Second Field Test." *Modern Language Journal* 58: 24–32.

Asher, J. 1977. *Learning Another Language Through Actions: The Complete Teacher's Guidebook*. Los Gatos, CA: Sky Oaks Publications.

Banjar, M. 1981. *The Effect of a Listening Comprehension Component on Saudi Secondary Students' EFL Skills*. Master's thesis in TESL; University of California, Los Angeles.

Blair, R. W. 1983. *Innovative Approaches to Language Teaching*. Rowley, MA: Newbury House.

Hill, J. 1970. "Foreign Accents, Language Acquisition, and Cerebral Dominance Revisited." *Language Learning* 20: 237–248.

Krashen, S., and T. Terrell. 1983. *The Natural Approach: Language Acquisition in the Classroom*. Oxford, UK: Pergamon Press.

Larsen-Freeman, D. 1986. *Techniques and Principles in Language Teaching*. New York: Oxford University Press.

Nida, E. A. 1971. "Sociopsychological Problems in Language Mastery and Retention." *The Psychology of Second Language Learning*, edited by P. Pimsleur and T. Quinn. Cambridge, UK: Cambridge University Press.

Postovsky, V.A. 1970. "The Effects of Delay in Oral Practice at the Beginning of Second Language Teaching." Ph.D. dissertation; University of California, Berkeley.

Postovsky, V.A. 1975. "On Paradoxes in Foreign Language Teaching." *Modern Language Journal* 59: 18–22.

Postovsky, V. A. 1976. "The Priority of Aural Comprehension in the Language Acquisition Process." *Proceedings of the Fourth AILA Congress*. Stuttgart: AILA Congress.

Sorenson, A. 1967. "Multilingualism in the Northwest Amazon." *American Anthropologist* 69: 670–684.

Winitz, H. n.d. "The Learnables." Kansas City, MO: International Linguistics Corporation.

Chapter Four

Praninskas, J. 1973. *Rapid Review of English Grammar*. Englewood Cliffs, NJ: Prentice-Hall.

Rassias, J. A. 1983. "New Dimensions in Language Training: The Dartmouth College Experiment." *Methods that Work,* edited by J. W. Oller and P. Richard-Amato. Rowley, MA: Newbury House.

Chapter Five

Carterette, E.C., and M.H. Jones. 1974. *Informal Speech.* Berkeley and Los Angeles: University of California Press.

Crookall, D. 1978. "The Design and Exploitation of a Role-Play/ Simulation." *Recherches et Echanges* 3: 1, cited in Stern.

Early, P.B. 1977. "Postscript to Games, Simulations, and Role-playing." *ELT Documents.* London: British Council English Teaching Information Center.

Guiora, A. 1972. "Construct Validity and Transpositional Research: Toward an Empirical Study of Psychoanalytic Concepts." *Comprehensive Psychiatry* 13: 139-150.

Heyde, A.W. 1979. "The Relationship of Self-Esteem to the Oral Production of a Second Language." *On TESOL '77—Teaching and Learning English as a Second Language: Trends in Research and Practice,* edited by H.D. Brown, C.A. Yorio, and R.H. Crymes. Washington, DC: TESOL.

Hines, M.E. 1973. *Skits in English as a Second Language.* New York: Regents Publishing Co., Inc.

Hinofotis, F.B. and K.M. Bailey. 1978. "Course Development: Oral Communication for Advanced University ESL Students." *Workpapers in Teaching English as a Second Language* 12: 7-19 (University of California, Los Angeles).

Hsu, V. 1975. "Play Production as a Medium of Learning Spoken Chinese." Paper presented at the Asian Studies on the Pacific Coast Conference. ERIC Document Reproduction Service: No. ED 112-667.

Mann, J. 1970. "The Present State of Psychodrama Research." Paper presented at the American Psychological Association Convention, Miami Beach. ERIC Document Reproduction Service: No. ED 943-055.

Moulding, S. 1978. "The Development of Appropriacy Through Drama Techniques." *Recherches et Echanges* 3: 1, cited in Stern.

Rosensweig, F. 1974. "Improving Communicative Competence of Advanced ESL Students." Master's thesis in TESL; University of California, Los Angeles.

Schumann, J. 1975. "Affective Factors and the Problem of Age in Second-Language Acquisition." *Language Learning* 25: 209–235.

Stern, S.L. 1980. "Drama in Second Language Learning from a Psycholinguistic Perspective." *Language Learning.* 30:1, 77–97.

Via, R. 1976. *English in Three Acts.* Honolulu: East-West Center, University Press of Hawaii.

White House Transcripts, The. 1974. New York: The Viking Press.

Chapter Seven

Celce-Murcia, M., and D. Larsen-Freeman. 1983. *The Grammar Book.* Rowley, MA: Newbury House.

Heaton, J. 1979. "An Audiovisual Method for ESL." *Teaching English as a Second or Foreign Language*, edited by M. Celce-Murcia and L. McIntosh. Rowley, MA: Newbury House.

Kelly, L.G. 1976. *25 Centuries of Language Teaching.* Rowley, MA: Newbury House.

Schumann, B. 1981. "Memory and Second Language Learning." Master's thesis in TESL; University of California, Los Angeles.

Chapter Eight

Johnson, K., and K. Morrow (eds.). 1981. *Communication in the Classroom.* New York and London: Longman.

Littlewood, W. 1981. *Communicative Language Teaching.* Cambridge, UK: Cambridge University Press.

Shaw, P. and J. B. Taylor. 1978. "Non-Pictorial Visual Aids." *Visual Aids for Classroom Interaction*, edited by S. Holden. London: Modern English Publications, Ltd.

Chapter Nine

Ciardi, J., and M. Williams. 1975. *How Does a Poem Mean?* Boston: Houghton Mifflin Co.

Dubin, F. 1974. "An Overlooked Resource for English Language Teaching: Pop, Rock, and Folk Music." Paper presented at the TESOL Convention, Denver, CO, on March 7, 1974.

Gasser, M., and E. Waldman. 1979. "Using Songs and Games in the ESL Classroom." *Teaching English as a Second or Foreign Language*, edited by M. Celce-Murcia and L. McIntosh. Rowley, MA: Newbury House.

Hulquist, M. 1984. "Activities for the Adult ESL Student, Level 3: a handbook for teachers." Manuscript; University of California, Los Angeles; TESL Program.

Kind, U. 1980. *Tune in to English*. New York: Regents.

Osman, A., and J. McConochie. 1979. *If You Feel Like Singing*. New York and London: Longman.

Perrine, L. 1977. *Sound and Sense*. 5th ed. New York: Harcourt Brace Jovanovich, Inc.

Pomeroy, C.A. 1974. *Songs for Intermediate ESL*. Master's thesis; University of California, Los Angeles.

Povey, J. 1979. "The Teaching of Literature in Advanced ESL Classes." *Teaching English as a Second or Foreign Language*, edited by M. Celce-Murcia and L. McIntosh. Rowley, MA: Newbury House.

Richards, J., and M. Poliquin. 1972. *English Through Song: A Songbook for English as a Second Language*. Rowley, MA: Newbury House.

Richards, J. 1969. "Songs in Language Learning." *TESOL Quarterly* 3(2): 161–174.

Shaw, A. M. 1970. "How to Make Songs for Language Drill." *English Language Teaching* 24(2): 125–132.

"Songs to Sing in Class." 1966. *English Teaching Forum*. Winter 4(4).

Chapter Ten

Brumfit, C. 1984. "The Bangalore Procedural Syllabus." *English Language Teaching* 38(4): 233–241.

Ford, C.K., and A.M. Silverman. 1981. *American Cultural Encounters*. San Francisco: Alemany Press.

Johnson, F.C. 1973. *English as a Second Language: An Individual Approach*. Singapore: Jacaranda Press.

Lee, W.R. 1979. *Language Teaching Games and Contests*. 2nd ed. New York: Oxford University Press.

McCallum, G. 1980. *101 Word Games*. New York: Oxford University Press.

Maley, A. 1981. "Games and Problem Solving." *Communication in the Classroom*, edited by K. Johnson and K. Morrow. London: Longman.

Rinvolucri, M. 1985. *Grammar Games: A Resource Book for Teachers*. Cambridge, UK: Cambridge University Press.

Rosenswieg, F. 1974. *Improving the Communicative Competence of Advanced ESL Students*. Master's thesis in TESL; University of California, Los Angeles.

Simon, S.B., L. W. Howe, and H. Kirschenbaum. 1972. *Values Clarification: A Handbook of Practical Strategies for Teachers and Students*. New York: Hart Publishing Co.

Widdowson, H. 1986. Plenary presentation at the TESOL Spain Conference. Madrid, April, 1986.

Wright, A., *et al*. 1984. *Games for Language Learning*. Cambridge, UK: Cambridge University Press.

Chapter Eleven

Chaudron, C. 1983. "Research on Metalinguistic Judgments: A Review of Theory, Methods, and Results." *Language Learning* 33:3.

Cohen, A.D. 1983. "Reformulating Compositions." *TESOL Newsletter* 17(6): 1, 4–5.

Cohen, A. D. 1985. "Reformulation: Another Way to Get Feedback." *The Writing Lab Newsletter* 10(2): 6–10 (Purdue University).

Dykstra, G., *et al*. 1966. *Ananse Tales: A Course in Controlled Composition*. New York: Teacher's College Press, Columbia University.

Goodman, K.S. 1970. "Reading: A Psycholinguistic Guessing Game." *Language Reading: An Interdisciplinary Approach*, edited by D. V. Gunderson. Washington, DC: Center for Applied Linguistics.

Goodman, Y.M., and K.S. Goodman. 1971. *Linguistics, Psycholinguistics, and the Teaching of Reading*. Newark, DE: International Reading Association.

Kirsner, R.S., and S.A. Thompson. 1976. "The Role of Pragmatic Inference in Semantics: A Study of Sensory-Verb Complements in English." *Glossa* 10(2): 200–240.

McGirt, J.D. 1984. "The Effect of Morphological and Syntactic Errors on the Holistic Scores of Native and Non-Native Compositions." Master's thesis in TESL; University of California, Los Angeles.

Paulston, C.B. 1972. "Teaching Writing in the ESOL Classroom: Techniques of Controlled Composition." *TESOL Quarterly* 6(1): 35–59.

Raimes, A. 1983. *Techniques in Teaching Writing*. New York: Oxford University Press.

Sawyer, J.V., and S.K. Silver. 1961. "Dictation in Language Learning." *Language Learning* 11(1–2): 33–42.

Schlesinger, I. 1968. *Sentence Structure and the Reading Process*. The Hague: Mouton.

Slager, W. 1973. "Creating Contexts for Language Practice." *TESOL Quarterly* 14(2): 71–79.

Smith, F. 1982. *Understanding Reading*. 3rd ed. New York: Holt, Rinehart and Winston.

Weschler, R. 1987. "An Inquiry Into Interview Analysis as a Fine Tuning Technique." Master's thesis in TESL; University of California, Los Angeles.

Wishon, G. E., and J. M. Burks. 1968. *Let's Write English*. Book 1. New York: American Book Co.

Witbeck, M. C. 1976. "Peer Correction Procedures for Intermediate and Advanced ESL Composition Lessons." *TESOL Quarterly* 10(3): 321–326.

Zamel, V. 1983. "The Composing Process of Advanced ESL Students: Six Case Studies," *TESOL Quarterly* 17(2): 165–187.

Conclusion

Gardner, R.C., and W.E. Lambert. 1972. *Attitudes and Motivation in Second Language Learning*. Rowley, MA: Newbury House.

Gattegno, C. 1976. *The Common Sense of Teaching Foreign Languages*. New York: Educational Solutions.

Hunter, M. 1974. "Piagetian Theory Applied to Assessment of the

Teaching Process." Manuscript; University Elementary School; University of California, Los Angeles.

Kelly, L.G. 1976. *25 Centuries of Language Teaching*. Rowley, MA: Newbury House.

Long, M. 1977. "Group Work in the Teaching and Learning of English as a Foreign Language." *English Language Teaching Journal* 31(4): 285–291.

Oller, J.W., A.J. Hudson, and P. F. Liu. 1977. "Attitudes and Attained Proficiency in ESL: A Sociolinguistic Study of Native Speakers of Chinese in the U.S." *Language Learning* 27:1.

Pica, T. 1985. "The Selective Impact of Classroom Instruction on Second Language Acquisition." *Applied Linguistics* 6: 214–222.

Pica, T., and C. Doughty. 1985. "Input and Interaction in the Communicative Language Classroom: A Comparison of Teacher-Fronted and Group Activities." *Input in Second Language Acquisition*, edited by S.M. Gass and C.G. Madden. Rowley, MA: Newbury House.

Snow, M., with R. Shapira. 1985. "The Role of Social-Psychological Factors in Second Language Learning." *Beyond Basics*, edited by M. Celce-Murcia. Rowley, MA: Newbury House.

·STRUCTURE AND WORD INDEX·

(to accompany *Techniques and Resources for Teaching Grammar*
by M. Celce-Murcia & S. Hilles)

186